How You Can Apply for
Social Security Disability Benefits

Diana Gadd

Macmillan • USA

Macmillan General Reference
A Simon & Schuster Macmillan Company
1633 Broadway
New York, NY 10019

Copyright © 1996 by Diana Gadd

All rights reserved including the right of reproduction in whole or in part in any form.

An ARCO Book

MACMILLAN is a registered trademark of Macmillan, Inc.
ARCO is a registered trademark of Prentice-Hall, Inc.

ISBN: 0-02-860599-3

Manufactured in the United States of America

10 9 8 7 6 5 4 3 2 1

Contents

	Preface	v
Chapter 1	SSDI versus SSI	1
Chapter 2	Understanding SSA and How It Evaluates Your Claim for Benefits	5
Chapter 3	Listing of Impairments—Part A	15
Chapter 4	Listing of Impairments—Part B	39
Chapter 5	Proving Your Inability to Work	73
Chapter 6	Supplemental Security Income (SSI)	79
Chapter 7	How to Complete Your Disability Application	93
Chapter 8	You've Been Approved!	129
Chapter 9	Reconsideration Appeal	137
Chapter 10	Administrative Law Judge Appeal	149
	Bibliography	167
	Index	168

Preface

Every year thousands of people apply for and are denied Social Security disability benefits. In fact, 70 percent of those who apply for benefits are immediately denied after filing their initial application.

This book was written to help people understand the entire Social Security determination process. Although individuals may obtain access to the official *Social Security Handbook* published by the U.S. Department of Health at their local federal depository libraries, many people are denied benefits simply because they do not provide all the essential information needed to prove their disability. After reading this book you will learn how to properly present your illness, medication, side effects, symptoms, and work history in your paperwork so that the Social Security Administration (SSA) understands your disability and you have a better chance of being awarded benefits.

Always keep in mind that you have to *prove* to SSA that you are disabled. These pages will help you bring all your information together so that you can properly present your case. Don't just read this book through once. If there is something you do not follow, reread it. Make sure you understand what SSA is looking for before you submit your paperwork for benefits. A little extra effort now will save you time in the long run.

This book will also take you through each phase of the appeals process. Although 70 percent of those who initially apply for Social Security benefits are denied, many of them—in fact, *60 to 70 percent* of them—could be awarded benefits if they follow through with their appeals. Remember, an individual who is approved for disability benefits stands to gain a monthly income source *plus* assistance with hospital and other medical costs. *It is worth the fight to follow through with your appeals!*

In addition, if you were previously denied Social Security benefits and are currently applying for a reconsideration or an administrative law judge appeal, it is recommended that you read this entire book and not just the section on appeals. By reading the entire book you might come across vital information that you left out of your original paperwork but can present now on the appeal level.

Also, don't forget to *keep copies of all your paperwork*. Once an SSA office in California caught fire and all of its files were lost in the rubble. Claimants subsequently had to resubmit all of their paperwork. It is extremely important that you keep a record of everything you send to SSA.

Lastly, remember to be *patient* when dealing with SSA. Getting approved is a long process, and constantly calling SSA will not speed it. This book, though, will help you avoid any needless delays by making sure you provide all the necessary data about your disability.

Chapter 1

SSDI VERSUS SSI

Any American citizen up to the age of 64 may apply for disability benefits. You must file a disability application while you are disabled or no later than 12 months after your disability ended. Social Security pays disability benefits under two programs:

1. Social Security Disability Insurance (SSDI), also called the Title II program
2. Supplemental Security Income Program (SSI), also called the Title XVI program

DO I QUALIFY FOR SSDI BENEFITS?

The disability benefits program that working adults most commonly qualify for is SSDI. Under SSDI, monthly awards are based on how much income was earned in the 40 quarters prior to when the disability began. A quarter is defined as a period of three months ending March 31, June 30, September 30, or December 31 of any year. During a telephone interview, a representative from the Social Security Administration (SSA) will review your earnings and generate a report that informs you if enough income was earned to qualify you for an "insured status." An insured status means a sufficient amount of income was made to enable you to apply for SSDI disability benefits. If you are not found to be insured, that means not enough income was earned to qualify you for SSDI benefits, and you will be applying for SSI disability benefits instead.

DO I QUALIFY FOR SSI BENEFITS?

To qualify for SSI benefits, you must be 65 or older, blind, or disabled, and you must not have sufficient income or resources to maintain a standard of living at the established federal minimum income level. The purpose of the SSI program is to assure a minimum level of income for people who are impaired, are unable to work, and have no other sources of income.

In some cases, if a person does not have a sufficient amount of income or resources, but has worked long enough to be insured under Social Security, that person may apply for SSI and SSDI at the same time. This is called a concurrent case. If a person is married and his/her spouse makes a substantial amount of income, that person will not qualify for SSI.

Besides eligibility, other differences between SSDI and SSI programs are listed below:

- Unlike SSDI, no disability waiting period is required under SSI. Because SSI payments are based on financial need, the presumption that a person has resources to handle short-term health problems does not exist.
- Under SSI, you may qualify for an immediate disability payment if your condition is obviously disabling and you meet the SSI income and resource limits.
- People qualifying for SSI benefits usually receive food stamps and Medicaid, which helps pay doctor and hospital bills.
- Different work incentive rules apply to SSI recipients. One difference is that cash benefits and Medicaid continue as long as the SSI income limits are not exceeded. With regard to SSDI, if a person earns more than $500 monthly, both eligibility and cash monthly payments may end.

Overall, however, both the determination process and the medical requirements needed to prove one's disability are the same for both SSDI and SSI. The main difference between the two programs is that eligibility for SSDI is based on the amount of income accumulated from prior work, while eligibility for SSI is based on financial need. SSI will be discussed further in chapter 6.

WHAT HAPPENS ONCE I APPLY FOR SOCIAL SECURITY DISABILITY BENEFITS?

When you decide you can no longer work because of an impairment, contact your local SSA office by phone. SSA will ask some preliminary questions and then forward Disability and Vocational Reports for you to complete.

Once you complete these forms with both your financial and medical history, SSA will determine your case type. Your local SSA office will then set a date for a telephone interview. Once you complete your telephone interview, a copy of everything discussed will be sent to you. Sign the copy and return it along with any other information that is requested to SSA. Once all your paperwork is received, it is then forwarded to the state Disability Determination Section (DDS), where your case is assigned to a claims examiner. All medical sources are then contacted to supply a report about your disability, and you may be contacted to submit additional information. If there is not enough medical information, you will be asked to visit another doctor at no cost to you.

You will be notified in writing if your case is denied. Your paperwork will then be returned to your local SSA office and held there for 60 days or until you request a reconsideration appeal. If you decide to appeal your case, you have 60 days from the date of your denial letter to submit an appeal form.

Once SSA receives all the completed appeal forms, it will send your case back to DDS, where it will be assigned to a different claims examiner. The claims examiner will reevaluate your case and request additional medical reports if you visited any new doctors since the submission of your initial application. You will be notified in writing if your reconsideration is denied, and you will then have 60 days to file an administrative law judge (ALJ) appeal.

The ALJ appeal is usually a face-to-face hearing with a judge. At this level you can appeal on your own behalf, hire an attorney, or use an authorized representative, who can be a friend or relative. After the hearing, the judge has 90 days to issue a decision. This process, however, can take longer if you present new medical evidence or if the judge feels more evidence is needed before making a decision.

If your appeal is denied again, it is recommended that you hire an experienced attorney to take the case to the Appeals Council level for review.

WHAT IF I'M CURRENTLY RECEIVING WORKERS' COMPENSATION OR STATE DISABILITY PAYMENTS?

If your doctor has informed you that your disability is going to last more than 12 months or that it is permanent, you should apply for your SSDI or SSI disability benefits immediately even if you are already receiving workers' compensation or state disability benefits. Don't wait until your benefits end to apply, since it will take at least six months for the initial SSDI or SSI paperwork to be processed. If you qualify to receive Social Security disability benefits, SSA will take into account any funds you received under either of these two programs when calculating your retroactive payments.

Chapter 2

UNDERSTANDING SSA AND HOW IT EVALUATES YOUR CLAIM FOR BENEFITS

This chapter will show you how SSA evaluates paperwork and determines if a person is disabled. Don't let the paperwork intimidate you—you are not going to have to write anything technical for SSA. All you need to do is provide as much detailed information about your disability as possible.

WHAT IS A DISABILITY?

SSA defines a disability as "the inability to do any substantial gainful activity by reason of any medically determinable physical or mental impairment (or combination of impairments) which can be expected to result in death or has lasted or can be expected to last for a continuous period of not less than 12 months." You must be unable to do your previous work or any other substantial gainful activity.

WHAT IS A SUBSTANTIAL GAINFUL ACTIVITY?

SSA defines a substantial gainful activity (SGA) as work that involves performing significant and productive physical or mental duties for pay. Any substantial gainful activity requires that you have the ability to:

- Walk, stand, sit, lift, push, pull, reach, carry, or handle
- See, hear, and speak
- Understand, carry out, and remember simple instructions
- Use your own judgment
- Respond to supervision, co-workers, and usual work situations
- Deal with changes in a routine work setting

SSA also considers your age, education, work experience, and residual functional capacity (discussed below) when evaluating your disability. Your disability, whether physical or mental, must be proved by medical evidence consisting of signs, symptoms, and laboratory findings.

When evaluating your disability, SSA will not consider any physical or mental impairment or any increase in severity of a preexisting impairment that arises in connection with your confinement in a jail, prison, or other penal institution or correctional facility for a conviction of a felony committed after October 19, 1980. SSA considers an offense a felony if:

- It is a felony under applicable law; or,
- In a jurisdiction that does not classify any crime as a felony, it is an offense punishable by death or imprisonment for a term exceeding one year

Your conviction will also invalidate any prior determination establishing a disability. You may become entitled to benefits upon release from prison provided you are suffering from a disability at the time.

What is Residual Functional Capacity?

Residual functional capacity (RFC) is composed of activities that you are still able to perform in a work setting despite your impairment. SSA uses your RFC assessment to determine if you can do other types of work. A limited ability to perform certain physical activities such as sitting, standing, walking, lifting, carrying, pushing, pulling, reaching, handling, stooping, or crouching reduces your ability to do past work and other work. A limited ability to perform certain mental activities such as understanding, remembering, carrying out instructions, and responding to supervision, co-workers, and work pressures also reduces your ability to do past work and other work.

APPLICATION REQUIREMENTS

To be considered a claim for benefits, an application must generally meet all of the following conditions:

- It must be completed on an application prescribed by SSA.
- It must be filed with SSA.
- It must be signed by the claimant or someone who may sign an application for the claimant.

WHEN IS AN APPLICATION CONSIDERED FILED?

An application for benefits or a written statement, request, or notice is considered to be filed on the day it is received by an SSA employee at one of his/her offices or by an SSA employee who is authorized to receive it at a place other than an SSA office. SSA will accept as the date of filing:

- The date an application for benefits or a written statement, request, or notice is received by any office of the U.S. Foreign Service or by the Department of Veterans Affairs regional office in the Philippines.
- The date an application for benefits or a written statement, request, or notice is mailed to SSA by U.S. mail in the event that the receiving date would cause a loss or lessening of someone's rights.
- The date an application for benefits is filed with the Railroad Retirement Board or the Department of Veterans Affairs.

DOES THE CLAIMANT HAVE TO BE ALIVE WHEN THE APPLICATION IS FILED?

A claimant must be alive at the time an application is filed; however, there are a few exceptions:

1. If a disabled person dies before filing an application, a person who is qualified to receive any benefits on the deceased's earnings record may file one. The application must be filed within three months after the month in which the disabled person died.
2. If a person who paid burial expenses for which a lump-sum death payment was made dies before filing an application for the payment, the application may be signed by a person who could receive the payment for the deceased's estate.
3. If a disabled person files a written statement showing an intent to claim benefits with SSA before his/her death, an application then may be filed:
   a) By or for a person who would be eligible to receive benefits on the deceased's earnings record;
   b) By a person acting for the deceased's estate; or
   c) If the statement was filed with a hospital, by the hospital if:
      - No person described in paragraphs *a* or *b* of this section can be located; or
      - If a person described in paragraphs *a* or *b* of this section is located but refuses or fails to file the application, unless the refusal is made to avoid any harm to the deceased person or the deceased's estate.

DAILY DIARY

It's a good idea for you to start a daily diary once you file your initial application. Your diary should contain detailed information about all of your doctor(s) appointments, including the doctor's name, address, phone number, date of your appointment, why you went, and any treatments you received. It is imperative that you keep track of everything that went on during each appointment, since your doctor will submit a summary of it to SSA. Once your DDS examiner receives this report, it will be included with the rest of your file used to make a determination on your claim. It's been found that sometimes what was said or done in a doctor's office is not accurately relayed to SSA. Your keeping a diary of appointments will help avoid any inaccuracies.

You should also keep a record of all medications you are taking, including their dosage. Note any changes in your medication by your doctor. In addition, keep a record of days you do not feel well, along with days you cannot attend work or cannot carry out a particular duty. Keeping track of this information will prove to be critical if you decide to appeal your case.

Lastly, note in your diary any contact you have with SSA. This should include a summary of any doctor's appointments SSA schedules for you.

MEDICAL EVIDENCE

You have to prove to SSA that you are blind and/or disabled by furnishing medical and other evidence. Based on the information provided, SSA will develop your complete medical history for at least the 12 months preceding the month in which you filed your application, unless there is reason to believe an earlier period is necessary or you say your disability began fewer than 12 months before you filed your application.

After you submit your application, SSA will make an initial request for medical evidence from your doctor(s). SSA will make one follow-up request if no medical evidence is received between 10 and 20 days after the initial request. The doctor(s) will then have a maximum of 10 days from the date of the follow-up request to reply, unless more time is requested. The medical evidence received by SSA must be complete and thorough and must clearly explain the nature of your impairment and its limiting effects for any period in question. It must also state the probable duration of your impairment and your ability to perform work-related physical and mental activities.

All medical reports submitted to SSA about your impairment must come from acceptable medical sources. Acceptable medical sources are licensed physicians, licensed osteopaths, licensed or certified psychologists, licensed optometrists, and medical facilities authorized to send SSA copies of medical records, such as hospitals, clinics, sanitariums, or health care facilities. Medical reports should include the following:

- Your medical history
- Clinical findings such as the results from physical or mental status exams
- Laboratory findings such as blood pressure or x-ray results
- A diagnosis that explains the nature of your impairment based on its signs and symptoms
- Any prescribed treatment(s) along with a prognosis and your actual response
- A statement about what you can still do despite your impairment(s), based on the medical source's findings

You can also provide information about your impairment from other sources such as public and private social-welfare agencies, practitioners such as naturopaths, chiropractors, and audiologists, and nonmedical sources such as family members and friends.

Once SSA receives all of your medical evidence, it will evaluate your case and determine if you are eligible to receive benefits. If SSA needs additional medical information, it will recontact your doctor(s). If what it needs is not found in the new medical evidence, SSA will ask you to attend one or more examinations at its expense. SSA will not request an examination until it has made every reasonable effort to obtain evidence from your own medical sources. Therefore, it is wise to make sure that all your medical records are submitted to SSA to avoid any unnecessary delays. If you refuse to provide medical evidence because of religious or personal objections to medical examinations or treatments, SSA will make its decision solely on the basis of the available information.

WHAT IF I CANNOT ATTEND A SCHEDULED SSA MEDICAL APPOINTMENT OR TEST?

If you have a valid reason for not attending a scheduled SSA appointment or test, you must inform SSA before the examination. Examples of valid reasons are:

- Illness on the date of the scheduled examination or test
- Failure to receive timely notice of the examination or test, or failure to receive any notice at all

- Failure to receive correct information about the physician involved or the time and place of the examination

Inform SSA immediately if your doctor tells you not to attend a scheduled examination. In many cases, SSA may be able to get the information needed another way, or your doctor may agree to another type of examination for the same purpose.

SYMPTOMS

Symptoms are descriptions of your impairment such as pain, fatigue, shortness of breath, weakness, nervousness, dizziness, blurred vision, speech disorders, hearing disorders, depression, and anxiety. In determining your disability, SSA considers all of your symptoms, including pain, and the extent to which your symptoms are consistent with medical signs, laboratory findings, and other evidence.

SSA will evaluate the intensity and persistence of your symptoms, along with the following:

- The extent to which your symptoms limit your capacity to work
- Location, duration, frequency, and intensity of your pain or other symptoms
- Treatment(s) received for relief of your symptoms
- Type, dosage, effectiveness, and side effects of any medication taken to alleviate your symptoms
- Other measures you use or have used to relieve your symptoms, such as lying flat on your back, sleeping on a board, etc.
- Other factors concerning your limitations and restrictions due to pain or other symptoms

SSA has to give proper weight to your descriptions of pain. When explaining your disability, make sure to indicate if you are suffering from pain by describing:

- The location and duration of the pain and whether it is sharp, dull, aching, etc.
- What causes the pain, such as standing, sitting, bending, etc.
- What relieves the pain

- The physical limitations associated with the pain
- Which medications help or stop the pain

MEDICATION

SSA considers how the intake of medication(s) affects your symptoms, laboratory findings, and your overall ability to function. When you complete your Disability Report, make sure to indicate all the medications you are taking, their dosage, and the prescribing physician.

Although medications may control the most obvious manifestations of your condition, they may or may not affect the functional limitations imposed by your impairment. If your symptoms are reduced by medications, SSA will determine if your functional limitations persist despite the improvement. SSA will also consider whether your medications create any side effects that may cause or contribute to your functional limitations.

You may be suffering from symptoms that have been caused by your medications. Make sure to report any unusual symptoms to your doctor. If your pharmacy does not provide a printout that summarizes the possible side effects of the medication(s) you are taking, purchase a book that provides these types of data. Educating yourself about the medicines you are taking will help you intelligently discuss any adverse effects you may suffer from them.

PRESCRIBED TREATMENTS

You must undergo prescribed treatment(s) if it can restore your ability to work. SSA will not find you disabled if you do not follow the treatment(s) prescribed without a good reason. Good reasons for not undergoing a treatment are:

- Medical treatments are contrary to the established teaching or belief of your religion.
- Surgery was previously performed with unsuccessful results, and the same surgery is again being recommended for the same impairment.
- Because of its magnitude or unusual nature, treatment is risky for you.

- Treatment involves amputation of an extremity or a major part of an extremity.
- The prescribed treatment involves cataract surgery for one eye while the other eye suffers from an impairment, thus causing a severe loss of vision that is not subject to improvement.

ALCOHOLISM

SSA recognizes that severe chronic alcoholism constitutes a disability. Once you prove that you have been diagnosed as an alcoholic, SSA will determine whether or not you have the ability to control your drinking and whether or not alcoholism prevents you from obtaining and maintaining employment. Be sure to indicate in your paperwork your history of alcohol use. It is not SSA's position to criticize you, so make every effort to tell them everything about your condition. If you've been arrested for being intoxicated in public or for driving while intoxicated, be sure to include this in your paperwork—these events are indicative of an individual who has lost the ability to control drinking.

Alcohol dependency affects a person's ability to understand and carry out instructions. It may also cause hostility, which can hamper your ability to interact and cooperate with supervisors, co-workers, and the public. Therefore, be thorough when explaining your alcohol problem and how it hinders you from working. Keep in mind, though, that a representative payee may be assigned to your case if SSA feels you may use your disability benefits to obtain alcohol. Representative payees will be discussed further in chapter 6.

BLINDNESS

SSA will consider you blind if it determines you have statutory blindness, which is defined by law as having a visual acuity of less than 20/200 or a visual field restriction to 20 degrees or less.

If SSA recognizes you as blind and you meet the insured status requirement, it may establish a period of disability for you regardless of whether you can engage in a substantial gainful activity (SGA). A period of disability protects your earnings record under Social Security so that the time you become disabled will not count against you when determining if you have worked long enough to qualify for benefits as well as the amount of your benefits. However, you will not necessarily be entitled to receive disability insurance cash benefits even if you are blind. If you are a blind person under age 55, you must be unable to do any substantial gainful activity in order to be paid disability insurance cash benefits. SSA will find you are eligible for disability benefits, even though you are still engaging in a substantial gainful activity, if:

- You are blind.
- You are age 55 or older.
- You are unable to use skills similar to those you used in any substantial gainful activity that you did regularly and for a considerable period of time. However, you will not receive cash benefits for any month that you participated in a substantial gainful activity. If the skills and abilities of your new work are about the same as those you used previously, you will also not receive any cash benefits.

If, because you are blind and age 55 or older, you become eligible for disability benefits even though you are doing a substantial gainful activity, you are entitled to a trial work period if:

- You later return to a substantial gainful activity that requires skills or abilities comparable to those required in the work you regularly did before you became blind or became 55 years old, whichever is later; or
- Your last previous work ended because of an impairment, and the current work requires a significant vocational adjustment.

If you are *under* the age of 55, recognized by the SSA as blind, and are not performing a substantial gainful activity, you will be eligible for disability benefits. But if you are carrying out a substantial gainful activity, you will *not* qualify for any benefits.

Chapter 3

LISTING OF IMPAIRMENTS— PART A

SSA maintains a Listing of Impairments that it considers severe enough to prevent a person from performing any substantial gainful activity and that fall under its rules of disability. Most of the impairments listed are permanent or are expected to result in death. Impairments that are not expected to end in death must have lasted or be expected to last for a continuous period of at least 12 months.

The Listing of Impairments is divided into two parts. Part A applies to individuals 18 years old and older and may also apply to those under the age of 18 who have a disease that affects both adults and children similarly. Part B (which is discussed in chapter 4) applies only to individuals under the age of 18. It contains additional medical criteria applicable in instances where Part A does not give appropriate consideration to childhood disease processes.

Keep in mind that the presence of your medical impairment on SSA's Listing of Impairments does not make you automatically eligible for benefits. Your disability must be supported by medical evidence that consists of symptoms, signs, and laboratory findings.

- Symptoms are your own descriptions of your physical or mental impairment. Your statements alone, though, are not enough to establish a physical or mental impairment.

- Signs are anatomical, physiological, or psychological abnormalities that can be observed apart from your statements (symptoms). Signs must be shown by medically acceptable clinical diagnostic techniques. Psychiatric signs are medically demonstrable phenomena that indicate specific abnormalities of behavior. They must also be shown by observable facts that can be medically described and evaluated.
- Laboratory findings are anatomical, physiological, or psychological phenomena that can be shown by the use of medically acceptable laboratory diagnostic techniques. Some of these diagnostic techniques include chemical tests, electrophysiological studies (electrocardiogram, electroencephalogram, etc.), roentgenological studies (x-rays), and psychological tests.

SSA will also consider medical opinions given by one or more medical or psychological consultants. If SSA requires you to take additional medical tests, it will send you to a doctor at *no cost to you.*

It is important to stress that you must work closely with your doctor throughout the entire disability determination process. Many technical medical terms that you will surely not recognize will be discussed in this and the following chapter—making it easy for you to feel overwhelmed. Sharing all the information needed to prove your disability with your doctor will enable him to provide you, and in turn SSA, all the necessary reports.

Be careful not to make any false statements in your paperwork. SSA adheres to the Social Security Act, which provides for criminal penalties for misrepresenting the facts or for making false statements to obtain benefits for yourself or for someone else.

The following list of impairments provides an overview of what SSA looks for when evaluating an impairment and determining if it is indeed a disability. Each listing details the symptoms and laboratory evidence you need to substantiate your disorder. Keep in mind that since everyone suffers from different symptoms, not all could be listed. The information in this and in the following chapter is provided simply to give you an idea of how SSA will evaluate your paperwork.

SSA classifies impairments into 13 body systems and disease groups:

1. Musculoskeletal system
2. Special senses and speech
3. Respiratory system
4. Cardiovascular system
5. Digestive system
6. Genitourinary system
7. Hemic and lymphatic system
8. Skin
9. Endocrine system
10. Multiple body systems
11. Neurological
12. Mental disorders
13. Neoplastic diseases, malignant (cancer)

1. Musculoskeletal System

Impairments that relate to the muscles and the skeleton. Disorders associated with this body system include:

- Loss of function due to amputations or deformities
- Disorders of the spine
- Fractures of the upper and lower limbs
- Arthritis

Loss of Function due to Amputations or Deformities
Symptom
- Pain

Evidence
- Pain must be associated with relevant abnormal signs or laboratory findings: detailed descriptions of the joints including range of motion, condition of the musculature, sensory or reflex changes, circulatory deficits, and x-ray abnormalities.

Disorders of the Spine
Evidence
- History of difficulties with the spine.
- Results from a physical examination and a roentgenogram.
- Description of the location and character of any pain.

- Description of any mechanical factors that incite and relieve pain.
- Description of any prescribed treatment, including type, dosage, and frequency of pain-relief medication.
- Description of typical daily activities supported with findings.
- Detailed description of orthopedic and neurologic examination findings. Findings should include a description of gait, limitation of movement of the spine given quantitatively in degrees from the vertical position, motor and sensory abnormalities, muscle spasms, and deep tendon reflexes.
- Documentation of any surgical procedures that have been performed, including a copy of the operative note and available pathology reports.

Fractures of the Upper and Lower Limbs
Symptoms/Signs
- Any loss of function
- Pain
- Circulatory deficits
- X-ray abnormalities
- Restrictions from performing certain daily activities
- Limitations of movement
- Muscle spasms
- Swelling, tenderness, and joint inflammation
- Deformities, etc.

If you are going to be evaluated by an SSA-appointed doctor and you are claiming disabilities in this area, the doctor will observe:

- Your inability to get on and off the examining table
- Your inability to walk on heels or toes, squat, or arise from a squatting position
- Any evidence of significant motor loss

In addition, the doctor may measure grip strength and joint motions, and he may perform both a seated straight-leg-raising test and a supine (lying on back, face upward) straight-leg-raising test.

Active Rheumatoid Arthritis and Other Inflammatory Arthritis
Evidence
- History of persistent joint pain, swelling, and tenderness involving multiple major joints.
- A physical exam showing signs of joint inflammation despite prescribed therapy for at least 3 months. The inflammation should cause significant movement restriction of the affected joints and clinical activity that is expected to last for at least 12 months.

Arthritis of a Major Weight-Bearing Joint (due to any cause)
Evidence
- History of persistent joint pain and stiffness.
- A physical examination that shows signs of marked limitation of motion or abnormal motion of the affected joint with:
  a) Gross anatomical deformity of the hip or knee such as subluxation (an incomplete dislocation), contracture (a permanent muscular contraction due to loss of muscular balance), or bony or fibrous ankylosis (stiffening of a joint). X-ray evidence should show significant narrowing of joint space, significant bone destruction, and limited ability to walk and stand.
  b) Failure to return to full-weight-bearing status following surgical arthrodesis or reconstructive surgery of a major weight-bearing joint, or a return is not expected to occur within 12 months of the surgery.

Arthritis of One Major Joint in Each of the Upper Extremities (due to any cause)
Evidence
- History of persistent joint pain and stiffness.
- A physical examination that shows signs of marked limitation of motion of the affected joints.
- X-ray evidence of either significant narrowing of joint space or significant bone destruction with:

a) Abduction and forward flexion (elevation) of both arms at the shoulders, including scapular motion, restricted to less than 90 degrees; or
b) A gross anatomical deformity such as subluxation (an incomplete dislocation), contracture (a permanent muscular contraction due to loss of muscular balance), bony or fibrous ankylosis (stiffening of a joint), ulnar deviation, and enlargement or effusion of the affected joints.

2. Special Senses and Speech

Disabilities that involve speech, vision, or hearing. Disorders associated with this body system include:

- Diseases or injury to the eyes
- Loss of hearing
- Deafness
- Vertigo
- Vestibular disorder

Diseases or Injury to the Eyes

Symptom
- Loss of central or peripheral vision resulting in the inability to distinguish detail and to move about freely

Evidence
- Results from visual testing

Loss of hearing

(Evaluated in terms of the person's ability to hear and distinguish speech)

Evidence
- Results of an otolaryngologic examination performed by or under the supervision of a qualified otolaryngologist or audiologist
- Results of audiogram that meets the standards of the American National Standards Institute (ANSI) for air- and bone-conducted stimuli

Deafness
Evidence
- Results from:
  a) Otolaryngologic examination
  b) Pure-tone air and bone audiometry
  c) Speech reception threshold (SRT) test
  d) Speech discrimination testing
- Copy of medical examination reports and audiologic evaluations.
- Records obtained from a speech and hearing rehabilitation center or a special school for the deaf. If these records are not available or are found to be inadequate, a current hearing evaluation should be submitted.

Vertigo
A sensation of irregular or whirling motion. Includes Ménière's disease.

Symptoms
- Hallucination of motion and a sensation of dizziness, occurring constantly or in sudden attacks. (It is important to differentiate vertigo from "dizziness," which is described as lightheadedness, unsteadiness, or confusion.)
- Nausea, vomiting, difficulty coordinating voluntary movements such as walking, and incapacitation, especially during acute attacks.
- Ménière's disease, characterized by violent attacks of vertigo, tinnitus (a ringing or whistling in the ear), and fluctuating hearing loss. Remissions are unpredictable and irregular, but may be long-lasting.

Evidence
- In regard to Ménière's disease, prolonged observation and serial reexaminations

Vestibular Disorder
Evidence
- Comprehensive neurootolaryngologic examination with detailed description of the vertiginous episodes, including notation of frequency, severity, and duration of attacks.

- Results from a Békésy audiometry.
- Vestibular function assessed by positional and caloric testing, preferably by electronystagmography.
- When polytomograms, contract radiography, or other special tests have been performed, copies of reports should be obtained in addition to reports of skull and temporal-bone x-rays.

3. Respiratory System

Impairments to the respiratory system that can result from irreversible loss of pulmonary functional capacity.

Symptoms
- Shortness of breath
- Coughing
- Wheezing
- Sputum production
- Hemoptysis (the spitting or coughing of blood)
- Chest pain

Evidence
- History
- Physical-examination reports
- Chest roentgenogram reports
- Pulmonary-function testing (required to provide a basis for assessing the impairment, once the diagnosis is established by appropriate clinical findings)

SSA may determine that you do not have enough medical history to show the pattern of your chronic pulmonary disease and that the existing evidence, including properly performed ventilatory-function tests (tests that measure the movement of air into and out of the lungs) are not adequate to evaluate the level of your impairment. If so, SSA may send you to a doctor to take exercise tests that measure arterial blood gases at rest and during exercise. Before ordering these tests, however, SSA will make sure that it has evaluated all of your evidence, including results from a chest roentgenogram, ventilatory-function tests, electrocardiogram, and a hematocrit (a device used to determine the relative volumes of blood cells and fluid in the blood).

In addition, when completing your paperwork, remember to include documentation of any hospitalization and/or visits to the emergency room. Asthma sufferers should note in their paperwork if their medication causes high blood pressure and if their medication includes prednisone. Prednisone can cause users to develop both prednisone dependency and Cushing's syndrome. Cushing's syndrome is characterized by weight gain, reddening of the face and neck, excessive growth of body and facial hair, raised blood pressure, osteoporosis, raised blood glucose levels, and mental disturbances. Other possible symptoms of prednisone use include a benign or malignant tumor of the adrenal glands.

4. Cardiovascular System

Impairments relating to the heart and the blood vessels or the circulation. Disorders associated with this body system include:

- Hypertensive vascular disease
- Ischemic heart disease

Hypertensive Vascular Disease
Evidence
- Severe damage to one or more of the four end organs: heart, brain, kidneys, or eyes (retinae). Must be supported with appropriate abnormal physical signs and laboratory findings.

Ischemic Heart Disease
Symptom
- Marked impairment due to chest pain

Evidence
- Description of the pain must contain clinical characteristics (crushing, squeezing, burning, or oppressive pain located in the chest).
- Describe specifically the character, location (throat, arms, chest), radiation, and duration of the pain, and responses to nitroglycerin or rest.

If SSA finds that you do not have enough medical documentation, it may ask you to undergo various exercise tests. For instance, you may be asked to do a continuous progressive regimen on a treadmill. However, you will not be asked to perform any kind of exercise testing if you are currently using medication that may cause a significant risk if you undergo stress testing and if you have any of the following conditions:

- Unstable progressive chest pain
- Congestive heart failure
- Uncontrolled serious arrhythmia (irregular heartbeat) or uncontrolled fibrillation (irregular twitching of fibers in the cardiac muscle)
- Second- or third-degree heart block
- Wolff-Parkinson-White syndrome
- Uncontrolled marked hypertension
- Marked aortic stenosis (narrowing of the aorta)
- Marked pulmonary hypertension
- Dissecting or ventricular aneurysms
- Acute illness
- Neurological or musculoskeletal impairments

In addition, SSA assesses the results of any surgery three months following the procedure. Assessment of the magnitude of the impairment following surgery requires adequate documentation of pertinent evaluations and tests, such as an interval history and a physical examination with emphasis on signs and symptoms that may have changed postoperatively, as well as x-rays and electrocardiograms. If treadmill exercise tests or angiography have been performed following the surgical procedure, results of these tests should be provided to SSA. SSA also requires documentation of preoperative evaluations (such as hospital records and coronary arteriographic reports) and a description of the surgical procedure.

5. Digestive System

Disorders of the digestive system are usually caused by nutritional problems, multiple recurrent inflammatory lesions, or complications brought on by diseases. Overall, digestive problems must be shown to persist on repeated examinations despite therapy and to last for a continuous period of at least 12 months.

Surgery of the intestinal tract (including colostomy or ileostomy) is not considered by SSA to preclude all work activity if the individual is able to maintain adequate nutrition and function of the stoma. In addition, dumping syndrome rarely represents a marked impairment that would last for 12 months.

Peptic ulcer disease with recurrent ulceration after definitive surgery ordinarily responds to treatment. Definitive surgical procedures are those designed to control the ulcer disease process. Simple closure of a perforated ulcer does not constitute definitive surgical therapy for peptic ulcer disease. A recurrent ulcer after definitive surgery must be demonstrated on repeated upper gastrointestinal roentgenograms or gastroscopic examinations despite therapy to be considered a severe impairment that would last for at least 12 months.

Two other disorders associated with the digestive system are:

- Intestinal obstruction
- Malnutrition

Intestinal Obstruction

When completing your paperwork be sure to include documentation of persistent or recurrent intestinal obstruction (blockage or clogging of the intestines).

Evidence
- Abdominal pain
- Distension
- Nausea
- Vomiting
- Persistent or recurrent systemic manifestations such as arthritis, iritis, fever, or liver dysfunction not attributable to other causes

Malnutrition

A malnutrition chart that SSA uses when determining malnutrition as a disability can be found on the following page. Even if your weight matches the corresponding height, it does not necessarily mean that you suffer from malnutrition. You must prove to SSA that you have other problems associated with malnutrition, such as weight loss caused by gastrointestinal disorders, malabsorption, malassimilation, or obstruction. In addition, you must also prove that your particular weight has lasted for at least 3 months despite prescribed therapy and is expected to persist for at least 12 months.

MEN			**WOMEN**		
Feet	Inches	Pounds	Feet	Inches	Pounds
5	1	90	4	10	77
5	2	92	4	11	79
5	3	94	5	–	82
5	4	97	5	1	84
5	5	99	5	2	86
5	6	102	5	3	89
5	7	106	5	4	91
5	8	109	5	5	94
5	9	112	5	6	98
5	10	115	5	7	101
5	11	118	5	8	104
6	–	122	5	9	107
6	1	125	5	10	110
6	2	128	5	11	114
6	3	131	6	–	117
6	4	134	6	1	120

(Height measured without shoes. Chart accurate as of 4/1/95.)

6. GENITOURINARY SYSTEM

Impairments that relate to the organs of reproduction and urination. Disorders associated with this body system include:

- Chronic renal disease
- Nephrotic syndrome
- Periodic dialysis
- Renal transplant

Chronic Renal Disease
Evidence
- History, physical examination
- Laboratory evidence that shows the deterioration of renal function

Nephritic Syndrome (Degenerative Disease of the Kidneys)
Evidence
- Description of extent of tissue edema (swelling), including pretibial, periorbital, or presacral edema
- If present, description of ascites (accumulation of fluid in the abdomen), pleural effusion, pericardial effusion, and hydrarthrosis
- Results of pertinent laboratory tests
- If a renal biopsy has been performed, a copy of the report of microscopic examination of the specimen
- Complications, such as severe orthostatic hypotension, recurrent infections, or venous thromboses, evaluated on the basis of resultant impairment

Periodic Dialysis
Evidence
- Severe impairment, reflected by renal function prior to institution of dialysis

Renal Transplant
The amount of function restored and the time required for any improvement depend upon various factors, including the adequacy of post-transplant renal function, incidence and severity of any renal infection, occurrence of rejection crisis, the presence of systemic complications (anemia, neuropathy, etc.), and side effects of corticosteroids or immunosuppressive agents. A convalescent period of at least 12 months is required before it can be reasonably determined whether the individual has reached a point of stable medical improvement.

7. HEMIC AND LYMPHATIC SYSTEM

Disorders associated with this body system include:

- Anemia
- Sickle cell disease
- Inherited coagulation disorders
- Leukemia
- AIDS

Anemia

According to SSA, any disorder associated with anemia should be evaluated according to the ability of the individual to adjust to the reduced oxygen-carrying capacity of the blood. A gradual reduction in red-cell mass, even to very low values, is often well tolerated in individuals with a healthy cardiovascular system.

Evidence

- Chronic anemia (hematocrit persisting at 30 percent or less due to any cause) with a requirement of one or more blood transfusions on an average of at least once every two months or an evaluation of the resulting impairment under criteria for the affected body system.
- Chronicity, indicated by persistence of the condition for at least three months.
- Laboratory findings must reflect values reported on more than one examination over that three-month period.

Sickle Cell Disease

Evidence

- Hematologic evidence.
- Documentation of any vasoocclusive or aplastic (incomplete development of essential blood components) episodes. Include a description of these episodes' severity, frequency, and duration.
- Documentation of any painful (thrombotic) crises that occurred at least three times during the five months prior to SSA's determination.

- Documentation of any extended hospitalization (beyond emergency care) that occurred at least three times during the 12 months prior to SSA's determination; chronic, severe anemia with persistence of hematocrit of 26 percent or less; or evaluation of the resulting impairment under the criteria for the affected body system.

Inherited Coagulation Disorders (Blood Clotting)
Evidence
- Documentation of appropriate laboratory evidence.
- Prophylactic therapy, such as therapy with antihemophilic globulin (AHG) concentrates, does not in itself imply severity. SSA considers a coagulation defect (hemophilia or similar disorder) a disability if it is accompanied by spontaneous hemorrhaging that requires a transfusion at least three times during the five months prior to SSA's determination.

Leukemia (Acute)
Evidence
- Initial diagnosis must be based upon definitive bone-marrow pathologic evidence.
- Recurrent disease may be documented by peripheral blood, bone-marrow, or cerebrospinal fluid examination. The pathology report must be included.
- Acute phase of chronic myelocytic (granulocytic) leukemia is considered under the requirements for acute leukemia. SSA considers acute leukemia a disability $2^{1}/_{2}$ years from the time of initial diagnosis.

Aplastic Anemias or Hematologic Malignancies (Excluding Acute Leukemia) with Bone-Marrow Transplantation
Considered a disability for 12 months following transplantation. Thereafter, SSA will evaluate according to the primary characteristics of the residual impairment.

AIDS
Symptoms
- Fever, night sweats
- Swollen glands (enlarged lymph nodes) in neck, armpits, or groin
- Fatigue, persistent cough
- Unexplained weight loss, loss of appetite

Evidence
- Specific defect in natural immunity against disease
- Susceptibility to variety of rare illnesses
- Description of clinical findings, including results from serological testing, microbiologic cultures, or tissue biopsy
- Identification of all symptoms and an explanation of their restriction on the ability to work.

8. SKIN
Skin disorders may become long-lasting impairments if they involve extensive body areas or critical areas such as hands or feet. Such disorders must be shown to have lasted, despite therapy, for a continuous period of at least 12 months.

Make sure to include in your paperwork information on your use of any high-potency drugs, especially since they can cause serious side effects. In addition, when describing your skin disorder make sure to address the following issues:

- Do you have any deformity that might be distracting to others in the workplace?
- Does your disorder cause you anxiety?
- Does your disorder hinder your handling ability? Is it contagious?
- Do you suffer from pain?

9. ENDOCRINE SYSTEM
Impairment to the endocrine system is caused by overproduction or underproduction of hormones that causes structural or functional

changes in the body. If a particular organ system has been affected by a primary endocrine disorder, SSA evaluates the affected area under the appropriate body system.

Disorders associated with this body system include:

- Thyroid disorder
- Hyperparathyroidism
- Hypoparathyroidism
- Neurohypophyseal insufficiency (diabetes insipidus)
- Hyperfunction of the adrenal cortex
- Diabetes mellitus

Thyroid Disorder
Evidence
- Progressive exophthalmos measured by exophthalmometry; or evaluation of the resulting impairment under the criteria for the affected body system

Hyperparathyroidism
Evidence
- Generalized decalcification of bone on x-ray study and elevation of plasma calcium to 11 mg per deciliter (100 ml) or greater; or a resulting impairment evaluated according to the criteria for the affected body system

Hypoparathyroidism
Evidence
- Severe recurrent tetany, or recurrent generalized convulsions or lenticular cataracts. Evaluate under the criteria for Special Senses and Speech.

Neurohypophyseal Insufficiency (Diabetes Insipidus)
Evidence
- Urine specific gravity of 1.005 or below that is persistent for at least three months
- Recurrent dehydration

Hyperfunction of the Adrenal Cortex
Evidence
- Evaluation of the resulting impairment under the criteria for the affected body system

Diabetes Mellitus
Evidence
- Neuropathy demonstrated by significant and persistent disorganization of motor function in two extremities resulting in sustained disturbance of gross and dexterous movements or gait and station; or
- Acidosis occurring at least on the average of once every two months, documented by appropriate blood chemical tests (pH or pCO_2 or bicarbonate levels); or
- Amputation at or above the tarsal region due to diabetic necrosis or peripheral arterial disease; or
- Retinitis proliferans—evaluate the visual impairment under the criteria for Special Senses and Speech.

10. MULTIPLE BODY SYSTEMS
Obesity (Long-Term)
Evidence
- Documentation of weight-bearing-joint pain and back pain
- Shortness of breath
- Fatigue or the inability to move about easily

The obesity table on the following page is used by SSA when determining obesity as a disability. Even though you might meet the weight standards in the chart, you must also suffer from problems associated with being overweight such as high blood pressure and limitations in walking or standing for long periods of time because of joint and back pain.

Men			**Women**		
Feet	Inches	Pounds	Feet	Inches	Pounds
5	–	246	4	8	208
5	1	252	4	9	212
5	2	258	4	10	218
5	3	264	4	11	224
5	4	270	5	–	230
5	5	276	5	1	236
5	6	284	5	2	242
5	7	294	5	3	250
5	8	302	5	4	258
5	9	310	5	5	266
5	10	318	5	6	274
5	11	328	5	7	282
6	–	336	5	8	290
6	1	346	5	9	298
6	2	356	5	10	306
6	3	364	5	11	314
6	4	374	6	–	322

(Chart accurate as of 4/1/95.)

11. Neurological

Persistent disorganization of motor function in the form of paralysis, tremor, or other involuntary movements frequently provides the sole or partial basis for decision in cases of neurological impairment. The assessment of a neurological impairment is based on how it interferes with locomotion and/or the use of fingers, hands, and arms. It is especially important in neurological cases to provide a detailed description of all symptoms suffered, such as problems with speaking, swallowing, and breathing.

Disorders associated with this body system include:

- Seizures
- Multiple sclerosis

- Cerebral palsy
- Convulsive disorders

Seizures
Evidence
- Description of the type of seizure, including its frequency and duration. Also describe tongue biting or other personal injuries caused by seizures.
- Note if your seizures are unpredictable. This would show SSA that it is unsafe for you to hold a job, particularly if your work includes driving a vehicle or handling dangerous machinery. (SSA might send you a Seizure Questionnaire to fill out. A sample of this form can be found in chapter 7.)
- Your doctor should indicate the extent to which your description of your seizures reflects his own observations. If a professional observation is not available, testimony of persons besides yourself is essential.
- Documentation of at least one electroencephalogram (EEG) is essential in epilepsy cases.

Multiple Sclerosis
Evidence
- Documentation of any motor function disorganization
- Documentation of a visual or mental impairment
- Results from a physical examination that show significant muscle weakness caused by a neurological dysfunction in the central nervous system that is known to be pathologically involved in the multiple sclerosis process
- Description of any fatigue
- Descriptions of frequency and duration of exacerbations, length of remissions, and permanent residuals

Cerebral Palsy
Evidence
- IQ of 70 or less
- Abnormal behavior patterns such as destructiveness or emotional instability
- Significant communication problems because of speech, hearing, or visual defects

Convulsive Disorders
Evidence
- Detailed description of a typical seizure, including information on the presence or absence of aura, tongue bites, sphincter control, injuries associated with attack, and postictal phenomena

12. Mental Disorders

SSA evaluates a mental disorder on the basis of medical evidence as well as the limitations the disorder may impose on an individual's ability to work and whether these limitations have lasted or are expected to last for a continuous period of at least 12 months. Symptoms that should be included in a claimant's paperwork include:

- Disorientation of time and place
- Short-term or long-term memory impairment
- Any change in personality
- Sudden mood changes, such as explosive temper outbursts
- Catatonic or other grossly disorganized behavior
- Incoherence, illogical thinking
- Loss of interest in almost all activities
- Decreased energy
- Difficulty concentrating or thinking
- Feelings of guilt or worthlessness
- Thoughts of suicide
- Manic syndrome, characterized by at least three of the following: hyperactivity; speech problems; difficulty in thinking; inflated self-esteem; decreased need for sleep; easy distractibility; hallucinations, delusions, or paranoid thinking; and a desire to be involved in activities that have a high probability of painful consequences

Mental Impairment
Evidence
- Clinical signs. These signs are typically assessed by a psychiatrist or psychologist and/or documented by psychological tests.

- Psychological-test findings. The findings may show that the impairment is intermittent or persistent, depending on the nature of the disorder.

SSA will send claimants to a psychiatrist if they have not had a psychiatric evaluation on their own. The psychiatrist as well as SSA will examine the following:

Restrictions of Daily-Living Activities
SSA wants to know the extent to which an individual is capable of initiating and participating in activities independent of supervision or direction. Examples of daily-living activities include:

- Cleaning
- Shopping
- Cooking
- Taking public transportation
- Paying bills
- Maintaining a residence
- Caring appropriately for one's grooming and hygiene
- Using telephones and directories
- Using a post office

Social Interaction
Social interaction refers to an individual's ability to interact appropriately and communicate effectively with other individuals. Impaired social functioning may be demonstrated by having a history of:

- Altercations
- Evictions
- Firings
- Fear of strangers
- Avoidance of interpersonal relationships
- Social isolation

In work situations, SSA will look at an individual's ability to interact with the public, respond appropriately to persons in authority, and respond appropriately to criticism. A person who is highly antagonistic, uncooperative, or hostile has marked restrictions in social functioning.

Sustained Concentration and Persistence
Sustained concentration and persistence refers to the ability to sustain focused attention long enough to permit the timely completion of tasks commonly found in work settings. Deficiencies in concentration, persistence, and pace are best observed in work and worklike settings. Major impairments in this area can often be assessed through direct psychiatric examination and/or psychological testing. Strengths and weaknesses in areas of concentration can be demonstrated in terms of frequency of errors, the time it takes to complete tasks, and the extent to which assistance is required to complete certain tasks. When evaluating a case, SSA will determine if an individual has the ability to:

- Carry out short and simple instructions
- Maintain attention and concentration for extended periods
- Perform activities within a schedule
- Maintain regular attendance and punctuality
- Maintain a routine schedule without special supervision
- Make simple work-related decisions
- Maintain a normal workday and workweek without interruptions caused by psychologically based symptoms
- Maintain a consistent work pace without an unreasonable number of rest periods

SSA also tries to determine if a person has the ability to be aware of normal hazards and how to take precautions, the ability to travel in unfamiliar places, the ability to use public transportation, and the ability to set realistic goals or make plans independently of others.

Information concerning an individual's behavior during any attempt to work and the circumstances surrounding termination of the work effort are very useful in determining the individual's ability or inability to function in a work setting. Therefore, it is very important to bring to SSA's attention when completing your paperwork how the person acted in the work environment. It is also important to describe in your paperwork the effects of any medication on an individual's symptoms and overall ability to function.

13. NEOPLASTIC DISEASES, MALIGNANT (CANCER)
Evidence
- Specify the site of the primary, recurrent, and metastatic lesion.
- If an operative procedure has been performed, include a copy of the operative note and the report of the gross and microscopic examination of the surgical specimen. (If these documents are not obtainable, then the summary of hospitalization or a report from the treating physician must include details of the findings at surgery and the results of the pathologist's gross and microscopic examination of the tissues.)
- Detailed explanation of the therapeutic regimen, including any drugs given, their dosage, the frequency of drug administration, and plans for continued drug administration. Also describe complications or other adverse responses to therapy such as nausea, vomiting, diarrhea, weakness, dermatologic disorders, or reactive mental disorders.
- Include a description of your mental state. Are you suffering from depression or anxiety?
- Indicate if you will have frequent hospitalizations or outpatient treatments. (If you are going to be undergoing frequent hospitalizations or outpatient treatments, you obviously won't be able to handle a job for long periods of time.)

Chapter 4

LISTING OF IMPAIRMENTS—PART B

This chapter contains medical criteria for the evaluation of impairments in children under the age of 18. For children, SSA breaks down the body into these 13 body systems and disease groups:

1. Growth impairment
2. Musculoskeletal system
3. Special senses and speech
4. Respiratory system
5. Cardiovascular system
6. Digestive system
7. Genitourinary system
8. Hemic and lymphatic system
9. Endocrine system
10. Multiple body systems
11. Neurological
12. Mental disorders
13. Neoplastic diseases, malignant

1. GROWTH IMPAIRMENT

A growth impairment may be disabling in itself or it may be an indicator of the severity of the impairment due to a specific disease process. A determination of a growth impairment should be based upon a comparison of the current height with at least three previous determinations, including length at birth if available. Heights (or lengths) should be plotted on a standard growth chart such as the National Center for Health Statistics Growth Chart. Include body weight and age. Height should be measured without shoes. Also, include adult heights of the child's natural parents and the heights and ages of any siblings. Providing this information will enable SSA to identify those children whose short stature represents a familial characteristic rather than a result of a disease.

Bone Age Determinations
Evidence
- Descriptive report of roentgenograms specifically obtained to determine bone age. The standardization method used must be cited.
- Views of the left hand and wrist, knee, and ankle when cessation of growth is being evaluated in an older child at or past puberty.

Growth Impairment
Evidence
- Considered to be related to an additional specific medically determinable impairment, and one of the following:
  a) Fall of greater than 15 percentiles in height, which is sustained
  b) Fall to height below the 3rd percentile, which is sustained

2. MUSCULOSKELETAL SYSTEM
Disorders associated with this body system include:

- Juvenile rheumatoid arthritis
- Deficit of musculoskeletal function due to deformity or musculoskeletal disease
- Disorders of the spine
- Osteomyelitis (chronic)

Juvenile Rheumatoid Arthritis
Symptoms
- Inflammatory signs such as persistent pain
- Tenderness
- Erythema
- Swelling and increased local temperature of a joint

Evidence
- When evaluating this disorder, SSA will be looking for persistence or recurrence of joint inflammation despite three months of medical treatment and one of the following:
    a) Limitation of motion of two major joints of 50 percent or greater
    b) Fixed deformity of two major weight-bearing joints of 30 degrees or more
    c) Radiographic changes of joint narrowing, erosion, or subluxation
    d) Persistent or recurrent systemic involvement such as iridocyclitis or pericarditis
    e) Steroid dependence

Deficit of Musculoskeletal Function due to Deformity or Musculoskeletal Disease
Evidence
- Walking markedly reduced in speed or distance despite orthotic or prosthetic devices
- Ambulation that is possible only with bilateral upper-limb assistance such as walkers or crutches
- Inability to perform age-related personal self-care activities such as eating, dressing, and maintaining personal hygiene

Disorders of the Spine
Evidence
- Fracture of vertebra with cord involvement (substantiated by appropriate sensory and motor loss); or

- Scoliosis (congenital idiopathic or neuromyopathic) with
  a) Major spinal curve measuring 60 degrees or greater;
  b) Spinal fusion of six or more levels (SSA considers this a disability up to one year from the time of surgery);
  c) FEV (vital capacity) of 50 percent or less of predicted normal values for the individual's measured (actual) height; or
- Kyphosis or lordosis measuring 90 degrees or greater

Osteomyelitis (Chronic)
Evidence
- Consistent radiographic findings
- Persistence or recurrence of inflammatory signs or drainage for at least six months despite prescribed therapy

3. SPECIAL SENSES AND SPEECH
Disorders associated with this body system include:

- Visual impairments in children
- Hearing impairments in children

Visual Impairments in Children
Criteria for Central Visual Acuity
- Remaining vision in the better eye after best correction is 20/200 or less; or
- For children below 3 years of age at time of determination:
  a) Absence of accommodative reflex;
  b) Retrolental fibroplasia with macular scarring or neovascularization; or
  c) Bilateral congenital cataracts with visualization of retinal red reflex only or when associated with other ocular pathology

Evidence
- When providing proof of central visual acuity, provide detailed eye examinations (preferably the standard Snellen test). If this cannot be provided in very young children, a complete description of the findings using other appropriate methods of examination should be provided. Also include a description of the techniques used for determining the central visual acuity for distance.

- Documentation of a visual disorder must include a description of the ocular pathology.

Accommodative reflex is generally not present in children under 6 months of age. In premature infants, it may not be present until 6 months plus the number of months the child is premature. Therefore, absence of accommodative reflex will be considered a visual impairment only in children above the age of 6 months.

Hearing Impairments in Children

SSA takes into account the fact that a lesser impairment in hearing that occurs at an early age may result in a severe speech and language disorder. In addition, if it is found that the use of a hearing aid can improve a child's condition, it must be demonstrated to be feasible, since younger children may be unable to use a hearing aid effectively.

Criteria for Hearing Impairments
- For children below 5 years of age at time of determination, inability to hear air-conduction thresholds at an average of 40 decibels (db) or greater in the better ear; or
- For children 5 years of age and above at time of determination:
  a) Inability to hear air-conduction thresholds at an average of 70 db or greater in the better ear; or
  b) Speech discrimination scores at 40 percent or less in the better ear; or
  c) Inability to hear air-conduction thresholds at an average of 40 db or greater in the better ear, and a speech and language disorder that significantly affects the clarity and content of speech and is attributable to the hearing impairment

Evidence
- Audiometric testing performed and copy of results. The pure-tone air-conduction hearing levels are based on American National Standards Institute Specifications for Audiometers, S3.6-1969 (ANSI-1969). Report should indicate specifications used to calibrate the audiometer.
- Finding of severe impairment will be based on the average hearing levels at 500, 1,000, 2,000 and 3,000 hertz in the better

ear, and on speech discrimination scores at 40 percent or less in the better ear.

4. RESPIRATORY SYSTEM
Disorders associated with this body system include:
- Pulmonary insufficiency
- Pulmonary manifestations of cystic fibrosis
- Bronchial asthma

Pulmonary Insufficiency
Evidence
- Include a copy of spirometric tests. Tests should not have been performed during or soon after an acute episode. Include an evaluation of the child's overall effort in cooperating and understanding directions. Also include a statement in the report if tests could not be performed or completed and explain why (for instance, the child may be too young).

Pulmonary Manifestations of Cystic Fibrosis
Evidence
- History, physical-examination report, and pertinent laboratory findings
- A confirmation based upon elevated concentration of sodium or chloride in sweat with a description of the technique used for collection and analysis
- If ventilatory-function testing cannot be performed, provide descriptions of the following:
   a) History of dyspnea on mild exertion or chronic frequent productive cough
   b) Persistent or recurrent abnormal breathing sounds, bilateral rales, or rhonchi
   c) Radiographic findings of extensive disease with hyperaeration and bilateral peribronchial infiltration

Bronchial Asthma
Evidence
- Progression of the disease despite therapy and documented by one of the following:

a) Recent, recurrent, intense asthmatic attacks requiring parenteral medication
b) Persistent prolonged expiration with wheezing between acute attacks and radiographic findings of peribronchial disease

5. CARDIOVASCULAR SYSTEM

Overall evidence for impairments to the cardiovascular system should include history, physical findings, and appropriate laboratory data. Reported abnormalities should be consistent with the pathologic diagnosis. The actual electrocardiographic tracing or an adequate marked photocopy must be included. Report of other pertinent studies necessary to substantiate the diagnosis or describe the severity of the impairment must also be provided.

Cardiovascular Impairment
Evidence
- Delineation of specific cardiovascular disturbance, either congenital or acquired. This may include arterial or venous disease, rhythm disturbance, or disease involving the valves, septa, myocardium, or pericardium.
- Documentation of the severity of the impairment, with medically determinable and consistent cardiovascular signs, symptoms, and laboratory data. In cases where impairment characteristics are questionably secondary to the cardiovascular disturbance, include additional documentation of the severity of the impairment (e.g., catheterization data, if performed).

Cardiomegaly (Enlargement of the Heart)
Evidence
- Chest roentgenogram (6 ft PA film) will be considered indicative of cardiomegaly if:
  a) Cardiothoracic ratio is over 60 percent at age 1 year or less, or over 55 percent at more than 1 year of age;
  b) Cardiac size increases over 15 percent from any prior chest roentgenograms; or
  c) Specific chamber or vessel enlargement is documented.

Hypertensive Cardiovascular Disease
Evidence
- Age and elevated blood pressure must correspond to the chart below and indicate one of the following:
  a) Impaired renal function
  b) Cerebrovascular damage
  c) Congestive heart failure

ELEVATED BLOOD PRESSURE

Age	Systolic (over) in mm	Diastolic (over) in mm
Under 6 months	95	60
6 months to 1 year	110	70
1 through 8 years	115	80
9 through 11 years	120	80
12 through 15 years	130	80
Over 18 years	140	80

6. DIGESTIVE SYSTEM

Disorders of the digestive system that result in disability usually do so because of interference with nutrition and growth, multiple recurrent inflammatory lesions, or other disease complications. SSA feels such lesions or complications usually respond to treatment. To constitute a listed impairment, a disorder to the digestive system must be shown to have persisted or be expected to persist despite prescribed therapy for a continuous period of at least 12 months. Intestinal disorders, including surgical diversions and potentially correctable congenital lesions, do not represent a severe impairment if the individual is able to maintain adequate nutrition, growth, and development.

Disorders associated with this body system include:

- Gastrointestinal impairments
- Liver disease (chronic)

- Chronic inflammatory bowel disease (such as ulcerative colitis or regional enteritis)
- Malnutrition

Gastrointestinal Impairments
Evidence
- Pertinent operative findings
- Radiographic studies
- Endoscopy
- Biopsy reports
- Documentation of a liver biopsy if one has been performed in chronic liver disease cases

Liver Disease (Chronic)
Evidence
- Must include one of the following:
  a) Inoperable biliary atresia demonstrated by x-ray or surgery
  b) Esophageal varices (demonstrated by angiography, barium swallow, endoscopy, or prior performance of a specific shunt or plication procedure)
  c) Hospital records documenting hepatic coma
  d) Intractable ascites not attributable to other causes, with serum albumin of 3.0 gm/100 ml or less
  e) Chronic active inflammation or necrosis documented by SGOT persistently more than 100 units of serum bilirubin of 2.5 mg percent or greater
  f) Where a liver biopsy has been performed in chronic liver disease, documentation of the report of the biopsy
  g) Hepatic encephalopathy

Chronic Inflammatory Bowel Disease
(such as Ulcerative Colitis or Regional Enteritis)
Evidence
- Intestinal manifestations or complications, such as obstruction, abscess, or fistula formation, which have lasted or are expected to last 12 months
- Malnutrition (discussed on the next page)
- Growth impairment

Malnutrition
Evidence
- Due to gastrointestinal disease, causing either a fall of 15 percentiles of weight that persists or the persistence of weight that is less than the 3rd percentile (on standard growth charts) and one of the following:
  a) Stool fat excretion per 24 hours:
     (1) More than 15 percent in infants less than 6 months
     (2) More than 10 percent in infants 6 to 18 months
     (3) More than 6 percent in children more than 18 months
  b) Persistent hematocrit of 30 percent or less despite prescribed therapy
  c) Serum carotene of 40 mcg/100 ml or less
  d) Serum albumin of 3.0 gm/100 ml or less

7. Genitourinary System
Disorders associated with this body system include:

- Renal disease (chronic)
- Renal transplant

Renal Disease (Chronic)
Evidence
- History, physical examination, and laboratory evidence
- Indications of the disorder's progressive nature or laboratory evidence of deterioration of renal function
- Persistent elevation of serum creatinine to 3 mg per deciliter (100 ml) or greater over at least three months, or reduction of creatinine clearance to 30 ml per minute (43 liters/24 hours) per 1.73 square meters of body surface area over at least three months
- Chronic renal dialysis program for irreversible renal failure

Renal Transplant
The amount of function restored and the time required for any improvement depends upon various factors, including adequacy

of post-transplant renal function, incidence of renal infection, occurrence of rejection crises, presence of systemic complications (anemia, neuropathy, etc.), and side effects of corticosteroid or immunosuppressive agents. According to SSA, a period of at least 12 months following surgery is required for an individual to reach a point of stable medical improvement. Therefore, an individual is considered disabled for those 12 months following surgery.

8. Hemic and Lymphatic System
Disorders associated with this body system include:

- Sickle cell disease
- Inherited coagulation disorders (chronic)
- Leukemia (acute)

Sickle Cell Disease
Evidence
- Hemoglobin electrophoresis
- Vasoocclusive, hemolytic, or aplastic episodes (musculo-skeletal, vertebral, abdominal), documented by description of severity, frequency, and duration
- One of the following:
    a) A major visceral complication in the 12 months prior to application
    b) A hyperhemolytic or aplastic crisis within 12 months prior to application
    c) Chronic, severe anemia with persistence of hematocrit of 26 percent or less
    d) Congestive heart failure, cerebrovascular damage, or emtional disorder

Inherited Coagulation Disorders (Chronic)
Evidence
- Repeated spontaneous or inappropriate bleeding, or hemarthrosis with joint deformity. Condition should be documented by appropriate laboratory evidence such as abnormal thromboplastin generation, coagulation time, or factor assay.

Leukemia (Acute)
Evidence
- Initial diagnosis of acute leukemia must be based upon definitive bone-marrow pathologic evidence. Recurrent disease may be documented by peripheral blood, bone-marrow, or cerebrospinal fluid examination. Pathology report must be included
- Individuals are considered disabled for:
    a) 2½ years from the time of initial diagnosis; or
    b) 2½ years from the time of recurrence of active disease

9. ENDOCRINE SYSTEM

Disability is caused by a disturbance in the regulation of the secretion or metabolism of one or more hormones that is not adequately controlled by therapy. SSA feels such disturbances or abnormalities usually respond to treatment. To constitute a listed impairment, these must be shown to have persisted or be expected to persist, despite prescribed therapy, for a continuous period of at least 12 months.

Overall evidence for impairments to the endocrine system should include history, physical findings, and diagnostic laboratory data. Laboratory tests will be considered abnormal if outside the normal range or greater than two standard deviations from the mean of the testing laboratory. Reports in the file should contain the information provided by the testing laboratory about its normal values for the relevant tests.

Disorders associated with this body system include:

- Hyperfunction of the adrenal cortex
- Adrenal cortical insufficiency
- Thyroid disorders
- Hyperparathyroidism
- Hypoparathyroidism or pseudohypoparathyroidism
- Diabetes insipidus
- Juvenile diabetes mellitus
- Iatrogenic hypercorticoid state
- Pituitary dwarfism
- Adrenogenital syndrome

Hyperfunction of the Adrenal Cortex
Evidence

- Growth retardation must be documented.
- Elevated blood or urinary free cortisol levels are not acceptable in lieu of urinary 17-hydroxycorticosteroid excretion for the diagnosis of adrenal cortical hyperfunction.
- There is unreponsiveness to low-dose dexamethasone suppression

Adrenal Cortical Insufficiency
Evidence

- Persistent low plasma cortisol or low urinary 17-hydroxycorticosteroids or 17-ketogenic steroids
- Evidence of unresponsiveness to ACTH stimulation
- Recent, recurrent episodes of circulatory collapse

Thyroid Disorders

- Hyperthyroidism with clinical manifestations despite prescribed therapy, and one of the following:
  a) Elevated serum thyroxine (T_4) and either elevated free T_4 or resin T_3 uptake
  b) Elevated thyroid uptake of radioiodine
  c) Elevated serum triiodothyronine (T_3)
- Hypothyroidism with one of the following, despite prescribed therapy:
  a) IQ of 70 or less
  b) Growth impairment
  c) Precocious puberty

Hyperparathyroidism
Evidence

- One of the following:
  a) Repeated elevated total or ionized serum calcium
  b) Elevated serum parathyroid hormone

Hypoparathyroidism or Pseudohypoparathyroidism
Evidence
- Severe recurrent tetany or convulsions that are unresponsive to prescribed therapy; or
- Growth retardation

Diabetes Insipidus
Evidence—Documented by Pathologic Hypertonic Saline or Water Deprivation Test
- One of the following:
  a) Intracranial space-occupying lesion, before or after surgery
  b) Unresponsiveness to Pitressin
  c) Growth retardation
  d) Unresponsive hypothalamic thirst center with chronic or recurrent hypernatremia
  e) Decreased visual fields attributable to a pituitary lesion

Juvenile Diabetes Mellitus Requiring Parenteral Insulin
Evidence
- One of the following, despite prescribed therapy:
  a) Recent, recurrent hospitalizations with acidosis
  b) Recent, recurrent episodes of hypoglycemia
  c) Growth retardation
  d) Impaired renal function

Iatrogenic Hypercorticoid State with Chronic Glucocorticoid Therapy
Evidence
- Resulting in one of the following:
  a) Osteoporosis
  b) Growth retardation
  c) Diabetes mellitus
  d) Myopathy
  e) Emotional disorder

Pituitary Dwarfism
Evidence
- Documented growth-hormone deficiency
- Growth impairment

Adrenogenital Syndrome
Evidence
- One of the following:
    a) Recent, recurrent self-losing episodes despite prescribed therapy
    b) Inadequate replacement therapy manifested by accelerated bone age and virilization
    c) Growth impairment

10. MULTIPLE BODY SYSTEMS

This section includes life-threatening, catastrophic congenital abnormalities and other serious hereditary, congenital, or acquired disorders that usually affect two or more body systems and are expected to:

1. Result in early death or development attainment of less than 2 years of age
2. Produce long-term, if not lifelong, significant interference with age-appropriate major daily or personal-care activities

Overall evidence for this body system includes:

- Confirmation of a positive diagnosis by a clinical description of the usual abnormal physical findings associated with the condition.
- Laboratory tests, including chromosomal analysis where appropriate (e.g., Down's syndrome).
- Documentation of immune-deficiency disease must be submitted and may include quantitative immunoglobulins, skin

tests for delayed hypersensitivity, lymphocyte stimulative tests, and measures of cellular immunity mediators.

Down's Syndrome (Excluding Mosaic Down's Syndrome)
Evidence
- Clinical findings, including characteristic physical features
- Laboratory tests such as chromosomal analysis

Multiple Body Dysfunction
Due to any confirmed hereditary, congenital, or acquired condition such as mosaic Down's syndrome, chromosomal abnormalities other than Down's syndrome, fetal alcohol syndrome, and severe chronic neonatal infections (such as toxoplasmosis, rubella syndrome, cytomegalic inclusion disease, and herpes encephalitis), with one of the following:

1. Persistent motor dysfunction as a result of hypotonia and/or musculoskeletal weakness, postural reaction deficit, abnormal primitive reflexes, or other neurological impairment. Also, significant interference with age-appropriate major daily or personal care activities. Such activities for infants or young children would include head control, swallowing, following, reaching, grasping, sitting, crawling, walking, and eating.
2. Mental impairment.
3. Growth impairment.
4. Significant interference with communication because of speech, hearing, or visual impairments.
5. Cardiovascular impairments.
6. Other impairments, such as, but not limited to, malnutrition, hypothyroidism, or seizures.

Catastrophic Congenital Abnormalities
Evidence
- One of the following:
    a) A positive diagnosis (such as anencephaly, trisomy D or E, cyclopia, etc.) generally regarded as being incompatible with extrauterine life

b) A positive diagnosis (such as cri du chat syndrome or Tay-Sachs disease) wherein attainment of the growth and development level of 2 years is not expected to occur

Hypogammaglobulinemia or Dysgammaglobulinemia
Evidence
- One of the following:
  a) Recent, recurrent severe infections
  b) A complication such as growth retardation, chronic lung disease, collagen disorder, or tumors

11. NEUROLOGICAL
Disorders associated with this body system include:

- Seizures
- Motor dysfunction
- Cerebral palsy
- Communication impairment

Seizure Disorder
Evidence
- Description of a typical seizure, including its frequency and any associated phenomena.
- Results from an electroencephalogram.
- Results from a neurological examination.
- Sleep EEG is preferable, especially with temporal-lobe seizures.

Minor Motor Seizures
Evidence
- Frequency of clinical seizures
- EEG pattern
- Age at onset

Myoclonic Seizures (Whether Infantile or Lennox-Gastaut After Infancy)
Evidence
- EEG pattern
- Age at onset and frequency of seizures

Motor Dysfunction

Motor dysfunction may be caused by any neurological disorder. According to SSA, motor dysfunction may be caused by static or progressive conditions involving any area of the nervous system that produces any type of neurological impairment. The impairment may include weakness, spasticity, lack of coordination, ataxia, tremor, athetosis, or sensory loss.

Evidence
- Description of neurologic abnormality (e.g., spasticity, weakness), as well as a description of the child's functional impairment (i.e., what the child is unable to do because of the abnormality)
- Description of a recent comprehensive evaluation, including all areas of affective and effective communication, performed by a qualified professional
- Any tests given to substantiate a diagnosis (if one was made), such as blood chemistries and muscle biopsy reports

Major Motor Seizures (monthly)

Evidence
- In a child with an established seizure disorder, the occurrence of more than one major motor seizure per month despite at least three months of prescribed treatment, and one of the following:
  a) Daytime episodes (loss of consciousness and convulsive seizures)
  b) Nocturnal episodes manifesting residuals that interfere with activity during the day

Major Motor Seizures (at least one episode)

Evidence
- In a child with an established seizure disorder, the occurrence of at least one major motor seizure in the year prior to filing an application, despite at least three months of prescribed treatment, and one of the following:
  a) IQ of 70 or less
  b) Significant interference with communication because of speech, hearing, or visual defect

c) Significant emotional disorder
d) Documentation of any significant adverse effects of medication interfering with major daily activities

Minor Motor Seizure Disorder
In a child with an established seizure disorder, the occurrence of more than one minor motor seizure per week, with alteration of awareness or loss of consciousness, despite at least three months of prescribed treatment.

Cerebral Palsy
Evidence
- Motor dysfunction (as described above), or less severe (but more than slight) motor dysfunction and one of the following:
  a) IQ of 70 or less
  b) Seizure disorder, with at least one major motor seizure in the year prior to application
  c) Significant interference with communication due to speech, hearing, or visual defect
  d) Significant emotional disorder

Communication Impairment
Evidence
- Associated with documented neurological disorder and one of the following:
  a) Documented speech deficit that significantly affects the clarity and content of speech
  b) Documented comprehension deficit resulting in ineffective verbal communication for age
  c) Impairment of hearing

12. MENTAL DISORDERS
There are significant differences between the mental disorder listings for adults and children, because mental disorders in children may have characteristics different from the signs and symptoms found in adults. This is partly because activities appropriate to children, such as learning, playing, maturing, and adjusting to school, are quite different from the activities appropriate to adults.

Childhood activities also vary widely throughout the different stages of childhood, which leads to considerable variation in the signs and symptoms of mental disorders among children of different ages.

As with all impairments, mental disorders must be documented by medical evidence consisting of symptoms, signs, and laboratory findings. Here, symptoms are complaints presented by the child. Psychiatric signs are medically demonstrable phenomena that indicate specific abnormalities of behavior, affect, thought, memory, orientation, development, and contact with reality. In addition, information from doctors and other professionals as well as nonmedical sources such as parents should be submitted. This additional information will help in establishing the consistency of the medical evidence and in determining how long the condition has persisted. Other rich sources of data include documentation from occupational, physical, and speech therapists, nurses, social workers, and special educators.

As in adult cases, severity is measured according to the functional limitations imposed by the mental impairment. The functional areas that SSA considers are:

- Motor function
- Cognitive/communicative function
- Social function
- Personal/behavioral function
- Concentration, persistence, and pace

Below are five separate age groupings, each with its own criteria that SSA assesses when determining a disability.

1. Newborn and younger infants (birth–1 year old)
    SSA assesses severity in:
    a) Motor development
    b) Cognitive/communicative function
    c) Social function
2. Older infants and toddlers (1–3 years old)
    SSA assesses severity in:
    a) Motor development
    b) Cognitive/communicative function
    c) Social function

3. Preschool children (3–6 years old)
   SSA assesses severity in:
   a) Cognitive/communicative function
   b) Social function
   c) Personal/behavioral function
   d) Deficiencies in concentration, persistence, or pace resulting in a frequent failure to complete tasks in a timely manner. Any motor abnormalities should also be documented.
4. Primary-school children (6–12 years old)
   SSA assesses severity in the same areas as for preschool children. However, testing instruments more appropriate to primary-school children should be used. Information regarding the capacity to function in a school setting should be submitted as supplemental information. School records and standardized testing, which are both excellent sources of information concerning function, should always be provided.
5. Adolescents (12–18 years old)
   The criteria for this age group correspond to those of primary-school children. Again, testing instruments more appropriate to adolescents should be used. Provide any information regarding the capacity to have stable and lasting relationships, cooperative working relationships in school or at a part-time or full-time job, and the ability to work as a member of a group. Note any behavioral problems in socializing such as isolation or any withdrawal signs.

The following pages feature criteria for specific disorders that SSA uses when determining a disability associated with mental disorders.

Organic Mental Disorders

SSA characterizes this disorder with abnormalities in perception, cognition, affect, or behavior associated with the dysfunction of the brain. History, physical examinations, or laboratory tests including psychological or neuropsychological tests demonstrate or support the presence of an organic factor judged to be etiologically related to the abnormal mental state.

The required level of severity established by SSA is met when the conditions in both *A* and *B* below are satisfied.

A. Medically document persistence of at least one of the following:
   1. Developmental arrest, delay, or regression
   2. Disorientation of time and place
   3. Memory impairment, either short-term (inability to learn new information), intermediate, or long-term (inability to remember information that was known sometime in the past)
   4. Perceptual or thinking disturbance (e.g., hallucinations, delusions, illusions, or paranoid thinking)
   5. Disturbance in personality (e.g., apathy or hostility)
   6. Disturbance in mood (e.g., mania or depression)
   7. Emotional liability (e.g., sudden crying)
   8. Impairment of impulse control (e.g., disinhibited social behavior or explosive temper outbursts)
   9. Impairment of cognitive function, as measured by clinically timely standardized psychological testing
   10. Disturbance of concentration, attention, or judgment
B. Select the appropriate age group to evaluate the severity of the impairment:
   1. For older infants and toddlers (1–3 years old), resulting in at least one of the following:
      a) Gross or fine motor development at a level generally acquired by children no more than one-half the child's chronological age, documented by:
         (1) An appropriate standardized test; or
         (2) Other medical findings
      b) Cognitive/communicative function at a level generally acquired by children no more than one-half the child's chronological age, documented by:
         (1) An appropriate standardized test; or
         (2) Other medical findings of equivalent cognitive/communicative abnormality, such as the inability to use simple verbal or nonverbal behavior to communcate basic needs or concepts

c) Social function at a level generally acquired by children no more than one-half the child's chronological age, documented by:
   (1) An appropriate standardized test; or
   (2) Other medical findings of an equivalent abnormality of social functioning, exemplified by serious inability to achieve age-appropriate autonomy as manifested by excessive clinging or extreme separation anxiety
d) Attainment of development or function generally acquired by children no more than two-thirds of the child's chronological age in two or more areas covered by *a, b,* and *c* above, as measured by an appropriate standardized test or other appropriate medical findings

2. For children (3–18 years old), resulting in at least two of the following:
   a) Marked impairment in age-appropriate cognitive/communicative function, documented by medical findings (including consideration of historical and other information from parents or other individuals who have knowledge of the child, when such information is needed and available) and including, if necessary, the results of appropriate standardized psychological tests, or, for children under age 6, by appropriate tests of language and communication
   b) Marked impairment in age-appropriate social functioning, documented by history and medical findings (including consideration of information from parents or other individuals who have knowledge of the child, when such information is needed and available) and including, if necessary, the results of appropriate standardized tests
   c) Marked impairment in personal/behavioral functions, as evidenced by:
      (1) Marked restriction of age-appropriate activities of daily living, documented by history and medical findings (including consideration of information from parents or other individuals who have knowledge of the child, when such information is needed and

available) and including, if necessary, appropriate standardized tests; or
  (2) Persistent serious maladaptive behaviors destructive to self, others, animals, or property, requiring protective intervention
 d) Deficiencies of concentration, persistence, or pace resulting in frequent failure to complete tasks in a timely manner

Schizophrenic, Delusional (Paranoid), Schizoaffective, and Other Psychotic Disorders

SSA characterizes this disorder with the onset of psychotic features, characterized by a marked disturbance in thinking, feeling, and behavior. This disorder also features deterioration from a previous level of functioning or failure to achieve the expected level of social functioning.

The required level of severity established by SSA is met when the conditions in both *A* and *B* below are satisfied.

A. Medically documented persistence, for at least six months, either continuous or intermittent, of one or more of the following:
  1. Delusions or hallucinations
  2. Catatonic, bizarre, or other grossly disorganized behavior
  3. Incoherence, loosening of associations, illogical thinking, or poverty of content of speech
  4. Flat, blunt, or inappropriate affect
  5. Emotional withdrawal, apathy, or isolation
B. Older infants and toddlers (1–3 years old) must meet at least one of the appropriate age-group criteria in paragraph *B1* on page 60. Children (3–18 years old) must meet at least two of the appropriate age-group criteria described in paragraph *B2* on page 61.

Mood Disorders

SSA characterizes a disturbance of mood as a prolonged emotion that covers the whole psychic life, generally involving either depression or elation, and is accompanied by a full or partial manic or depressive syndrome.

The required level of severity established by SSA is met when the conditions in both *A* and *B* below are satisfied.

A. Medically documented persistence, either continuous or intermittent, of one of the following:
   1. Major depressive syndrome, characterized by at least five of the following, which must include either *a* or *b:*
      a) Depressed or irritable mood
      b) Markedly diminished interest or pleasure in almost all activities
      c) Appetite or weight increase or decrease, or failure to make expected weight gains
      d) Sleep disturbance
      e) Psychomotor agitation or retardation
      f) Fatigue or loss of energy
      g) Feelings of worthlessness or guilt
      h) Difficulty thinking or concentrating
      i) Suicidal thoughts or acts
      j) Hallucinations, delusions, or paranoid thinking
   2. Manic syndrome, characterized by elevated, expansive, or irritable mood, and at least three of the following:
      a) Increased activity or psychomotor agitation
      b) Increased talkativeness or pressure of speech
      c) Flight of ideas or subjectively experienced racing thoughts
      d) Inflated self-esteem or grandiosity
      e) Decreased need for sleep
      f) Easy distractibility
      g) Involvement in activities that have a high potential of painful consequences that are not recognized
      h) Hallucinations, delusions, or paranoid thinking
   3. Bipolar or cyclothymic syndrome with a history of episodic periods manifested by the full symptomatic picture of both manic and depressive syndromes (and currently or most recently characterized by the full or partial symptomatic picture of either or both syndromes)

B. For older infants and toddlers (1–3 years old), resulting in at least one of the appropriate age-group criteria in paragraph *B1* on page 60; or, for children (3–18 years old), resulting in at least two of the appropriate age-group criteria in paragraph *B2* on page 61.

Mental Retardation

This disorder is characterized by significant subaverage general intellectual functioning with deficits in adaptive functioning.

The required level of severity established by SSA is met when the conditions in *A, B, C, D, E,* or *F* below are satisfied.

A. For older infants and toddlers (1–3 years old), resulting in at least one of the appropriate age-group criteria in paragraph *B1* on page 60; or, for children (3–18 years old), resulting in at least two of the appropriate age-group criteria in paragraph *B2* on page 61

B. Mental incapacity, evidenced by dependence upon others for personal needs (grossly in excess of age-appropriate dependence), and the inability to follow directions so that the use of standardized measures of intellectual functioning is precluded

C. A valid verbal, performance, or full-scale IQ of 59 or less

D. A valid verbal, performance, or full-scale IQ of 60 through 70 and a physical or other mental impairment imposing additional and significant limitation of function

E. A valid verbal, performance, or full-scale IQ of 60 through 70 and:
   1. For older infants and toddlers (1–3 years old), resulting in attainment of development or function generally acquired by children no more than two-thirds of the child's chronological age in either paragraphs *B1a* or *B1c* on pages 60–61; or
   2. For children (3–18 years old), resulting in at least one of paragraphs *B2b, B2c,* or *B2d* on pages 61–62

F. Select the appropriate age group:
   1. For older infants and toddlers (1–3 years old), resulting in attainment of development or function generally acquired by children no more than two-thirds of the child's chronological age in paragraph *B1b* on page 60, and a physical or other mental impairment imposing additional and significant limitations of function

2. For children (3–18 years old), resulting in the satisfaction of *B2a* on page 61, and a physical or other mental impairment imposing additional and significant limitations of function.

Anxiety Disorders
In these disorders, anxiety is either the predominant disturbance or is experienced if the individual attempts to master symptoms, e.g., confronting the dreaded object or situation in a phobic disorder, attempting to go to school in a separation anxiety disorder, resisting the obsessions or compulsions in an obsessive-compulsive disorder, or confronting strangers or peers in an avoidant disorder.

The required level of severity established by SSA is met when the conditions in both *A* and *B* below are satisfied.

A. Medically documented findings of at least one of the following:
 1. Excessive anxiety manifested when the child is separated, or separation is threatened, from a parent or parent surrogate
 2. Excessive and persistent avoidance of strangers
 3. Persistent unrealistic or excessive anxiety and worry (apprehensive expectation), accompanied by motor tension, autonomic hyperactivity, or vigilance and scanning
 4. Persistent irrational fear of a specific object, activity, or situation that results in a compelling desire to avoid the dreaded object, activity, or situation
 5. Recurrent severe panic attacks, manifested by a sudden unpredictable onset of intense apprehension, fear, or terror, often with a sense of impending doom, occurring on the average of at least once a week
 6. Recurrent obsessions or compulsions, which are a source of marked distress
 7. Recurrent and intrusive recollections of a traumatic experience, including dreams, which are a source of marked distress
B. For older infants and toddlers (1–3 years old), resulting in at least one of the appropriate age-group criteria in paragraph *B1* on page 60; or, for children (3–18 years old), resulting in at least two of the appropriate age-group criteria in paragraph *B2* on page 61.

Somatoform, Eating, and Tic Disorders

SSA states "These disorders are manifested by physical symptoms for which there are no demonstrable organic findings or known physiologic mechanisms; or eating or tic disorders with physical manifestations."

The required level of severity established by SSA is met when the conditions in both *A* and *B* below are satisfied.

A. Medically documented findings of one of the following:
  1. An unrealistic fear and perception of fatness despite being underweight, and persistent refusal to maintain a body weight that is greater than 85 percent of the average weight for height and age, as shown in the most recent edition of the *Nelson Textbook of Pediatrics*
  2. Persistent and recurrent involuntary, repetitive, rapid, purposeless motor movements affecting multiple muscle groups with multiple vocal tics
  3. Persistent nonorganic disturbance of one of the following:
     a) Vision
     b) Speech
     c) Hearing
     d) Use of a limb
     e) Movement and its control (e.g., coordination disturbance or psychogenic seizures)
     f) Sensation (diminished or heightened)
     g) Digestion or elimination
  4. Preoccupation with a belief that one has a serious disease or injury.
B. For older infants and toddlers (1–3 years old), resulting in at least one of the appropriate age-group criteria in paragraph *B1* on page 60; or, for children (3–18 years old), resulting in at least two of the appropriate age-group criteria in paragraph *B2* on page 61.

Personality Disorders

SSA states these disorders are manifested by pervasive, inflexible, and maladaptive personality traits that are typical of the child's long-term functioning and not limited to discrete episodes of illness.

The required level of severity established by SSA is met when the conditions in both *A* and *B* below are satisfied.

A. Deeply ingrained, maladaptive patterns of behavior, associated with one of the following:
   1. Seclusiveness or autistic thinking
   2. Pathologically inappropriate suspiciousness or hostility
   3. Oddities of thought, perception, speech, and behavior
   4. Persistent disturbances of mood or affect
   5. Pathological dependence, passivity, or aggressiveness
   6. Intense and unstable interpersonal relationships and impulsive and exploitative behavior
   7. Pathological perfectionism and inflexibility
B. For older infants and toddlers (1–3 years old), resulting in at least one of the appropriate age-group criteria in paragraph *B1* on page 60; or, for children (3–18 years old), resulting in at least two of the appropriate age-group criteria in paragraph *B2* on page 61.

Psychoactive Substance Dependence Disorders

These disorders, according to SSA, are manifested by a cluster of cognitive, behavioral, and physiologic symptoms that indicates an impaired control of psychoactive-substance use with continued use of the substance despite adverse consequences.

The required level of severity established by SSA is met when the conditions in both *A* and *B* below are satisfied.

A. Medically documented findings of at least *four* of the following:
   1. Substance taken in larger amounts or over a longer period than intended, with a great deal of time spent recovering from its effects
   2. Two or more unsuccessful efforts to cut down or control use
   3. Frequent intoxication or withdrawal symptoms, interfering with major role obligations
   4. Continued use despite persistent or recurring social, psychological, or physical problems

5. Tolerance, as characterized by the requirement for markedly increased amounts of substance in order to achieve intoxication
   6. Substance taken to relieve or avoid withdrawal symptoms
B. For older infants and toddlers (1–3 years old), resulting in at least one of the appropriate age-group criteria in paragraph *B1* on page 60; or, for children (3–18 years old), resulting in at least two of the appropriate age-group criteria in paragraph *B2* on page 61.

Autistic Disorder and Other Pervasive Developmental Disorders

These disorders, according to SSA, are characterized by qualitative deficits in the development of reciprocal social interaction, in the development of verbal and nonverbal communication skills, and in imaginative activity. Often, there is a markedly restricted repertoire of activities and interests, which frequently are stereotyped and repetitive.

The required level of severity established by SSA is met when the conditions in both *A* and *B* below are satisfied.

A. Medically documented findings of the following:
   1. For autistic disorder, all of the following:
      a) Qualitative deficits in the development of reciprocal social interaction
      b) Qualitative deficits in verbal and nonverbal communication and in imaginative activity
      c) Markedly restricted repertoire of activities and interests
   2. For pervasive developmental disorders, both of the following:
      a) Qualitative deficits in the development of social interaction
      b) Qualitative deficits in verbal and nonverbal communication and in imaginative activity
B. For older infants and toddlers (1–3 years old), resulting in at least one of the appropriate age-group criteria in paragraph *B1* on page 60, or, for children (3–18 years old), resulting in at least two of the appropriate age-group criteria in paragraphs *B2* on page 61.

Attention Deficit Hyperactivity Disorder

Developmentally inappropriate degrees of inattention, impulsiveness, and hyperactivity characterize this disorder.

The required level of severity established by SSA is met when the conditions in both *A* and *B* below are satisfied.

- A. Medically documented findings of all three of the following:
   1. Marked inattention
   2. Marked impulsiveness
   3. Marked hyperactivity
- B. For older infants and toddlers (1–3 years old), resulting in at least one of the appropriate age-group criteria in paragraph *B1* on page 60; or, for children (3–18 years old), resulting in at least two of the appropriate age-group criteria in paragraph *B2* on page 61.

Developmental and Emotional Disorders of Newborn and Younger Infants (Birth to Attainment of Age 1)

According to SSA, developmental or emotional disorders of infancy are evidenced by a deficit or lag in the areas of motor, cognitive/communicative, or social functioning. These disorders may be related either to organic or to functional factors or to a combination of these factors.

The required level of severity established by SSA is met when the conditions in *A, B, C, D,* or *E* below are satisfied.

- A. Cognitive/communicative functioning generally acquired by children no more than one-half the child's chronological age, as documented by appropriate medical findings (e.g., in infants 0–6 months, markedly diminished variation in the production or imitation of sounds and severe feeding abnormality, such as problems with sucking, swallowing, or chewing), including, if necessary, a standardized test
- B. Motor development generally acquired by children no more than one-half the child's chronological age, documented by appropriate medical findings, including, if necessary, a standardized test

C. Apathy, overexcitability, or fearfulness, demonstrated by an absent or grossly excessive response to one of the following:
   1. Visual stimulation
   2. Auditory stimulation
   3. Tactile stimulation
D. Failure to sustain social interaction on an ongoing, reciprocal basis as evidenced by one of the following:
   1. Inability by 6 months to participate in vocal, visual, and motoric exchanges (including facial expressions)
   2. Failure by 9 months to communicate basic emotional responses, such as cuddling or exhibiting protest or anger
   3. Failure to attend to the caregiver's voice or face or to explore an inanimate object for a period of time appropriate to the infant's age
E. Attainment of development or function generally acquired by children no more than two-thirds of the child's chronological age in two or more areas (i.e., cognitive/communicative, motor, or social), documented by appropriate medical findings, including, if necessary, standardized testing

13. Neoplastic Diseases, Malignant

Disability determination in a growing and developing child with a malignant neoplastic disease is based upon the combined effects of:

1. Pathophysiology, histology, and natural history of the tumor
2. Effects of the currently employed aggressive multimodal therapeutic regimens

Combinations of surgery, radiation, and chemotherapy or prolonged therapeutic schedules impart significant additional morbidity to the child during the period of greatest risk from the tumor itself. This period of highest risk and greatest therapeutically induced morbidity defines the limits of disability for most childhood neoplastic diseases.

Evidence
- Diagnosis of neoplasm should be established on the basis of symptoms, signs, and laboratory findings.

- Site of the primary, recurrent, and metastatic lesions must be specified in all cases of malignant neoplastic diseases.
- If an operative procedure has been performed, evidence should include a copy of the operative note and the report of the gross and microscopic examination of the surgical specimen, along with all pertinent laboratory and x-ray reports.
- Also include a recent report directed especially at describing whether there is evidence of local or regional recurrence, soft part or skeletal metastases, and significant post-therapeutic residuals.

The following are additional criteria for some neoplastic disorders.

Lymphoreticular Malignant Neoplasm

Hodgkin's disease with progressive disease not controlled by prescribed therapy or Non-Hodgkin's lymphoma. Both are considered a disability for:

- 2½ years from time of initial diagnosis; or
- 2½ years from time of recurrence of active disease

Malignant Solid Tumors

Considered a disability for:

- 2 years from time of initial diagnosis; or
- 2 years from time of recurrence of active disease

Neuroblastoma

Evidence
- One of the following:
    a) Extension across the midline
    b) Distant metastases
    c) Recurrence
    d) Onset at age 1 or older

Retinoblastoma
Evidence
- One of the following:
  a) Bilateral involvement
  b) Metastases
  c) Extension beyond the orbit
  d) Recurrence

Chapter 5

PROVING YOUR INABILITY TO WORK

The previous two chapters dealt with the medical evidence claimants need to prove they are disabled. After evaluating all of the medical data, SSA examines an individual's work history and current job skills. Remember, to qualify for disability benefits you must prove that you cannot perform any type of work.

SSA will compare your residual functional capacity (the activities you are still able to do despite your impairment) with the types of work you performed in the past. You will not be found disabled if you have the ability to do your past work. If you are unable to do your past work, SSA will determine if you are able to do other work by examining three factors: age, education, and work experience.

Age

SSA examines the extent to which your age affects your ability to adapt to a new work situation. If you are unemployed solely because of your age, you will not be found disabled. However, age is considered a debilitating factor for anyone between the ages of 50 and 54 with a severe impairment and limited work experience. The age considered by SSA most significantly to affect a person's ability to perform substantial gainful activity is 55 years old and over. If you are severely impaired and age 55 or over, you will not be found able to work unless you have skills that can be used in less demanding jobs. If you are close to retirement age (ages 60 to 64) and have a severe impairment, SSA will not consider you able to adjust to sedentary or light work unless you have skills that are highly marketable.

You will not be asked to prove your age unless a determination on your claim or the amount of your benefits relies on knowing your exact age. If asked to prove your age, you will need to submit one of the following:

- Birth certificate
- Hospital birth record recorded before age 5
- Religious record that shows your date of birth and was recorded before age 5

If you cannot obtain one of the items listed above, you will be asked to submit one or more of the following that shows your date of birth or age:

- Original family Bible or family record
- School records
- Census records
- Statement signed by the physician or midwife who was present at your birth
- Insurance policies
- Marriage record
- Passport
- Employment record
- Delayed birth certificate
- Your child's birth certificate
- Immigration or naturalization record

EDUCATION

Information about a person's educational history helps SSA determine his/her reasoning ability, communication skills, and arithmetic ability. A lack of education does not mean you are unintelligent, but it might hinder you from working at other jobs. In your Disability

Report portion of your paperwork, you will be asked to write down the highest grade level of school you've completed. Your grade level is then categorized into one of the classifications listed below, used by SSA to determine the types of work claimants can perform:

- *Illiteracy*—little or no formal schooling.
- *Marginal education*—formal schooling at sixth-grade level or less. In this category, an individual usually has developed enough reasoning, arithmetic, and language skills to do simple, unskilled types of jobs.
- *Limited education*—seventh- through eleventh-grade level. An individual in this category has developed more skills than individuals in the marginal-education category, but still not enough to perform semiskilled or skilled jobs.
- *High school education and above*—twelfth-grade level or above. SSA considers an individual in this category able to do semi-skilled and skilled work.

The term *education* also includes how well you are able to communicate in English, since this ability is often acquired or improved through schooling. Since English is the dominant language in the United States, it is difficult for someone who doesn't speak and understand English to work in this country, regardless of the amount of education that person may have in another language.

WORK EXPERIENCE

Your work experience shows the kinds of skills you've acquired over the years. If SSA determines that you cannot use your skills in skilled or semiskilled work, your work background will be considered unskilled. If you have no work experience, SSA may consider you able to do unskilled work, since such work requires little or no judgment and can be learned in a short period of time.

SSA evaluates only the jobs you have had in the last 15 years. However, if you have a sixth-grade education or less and did only unskilled labor for 35 years or more, you will have to provide SSA information about all of the jobs you held since you began to work. In both your Disability and Vocational Reports, you will be asked to supply the following data about your work experience:

- The dates you worked
- Amount of days per week you worked
- Amount of hours per day you worked
- The wage you received
- If any, the kinds of tools, machinery, and equipment you used
- A description of how much walking, standing, sitting, lifting, and carrying you did during a working day, as well as any other physical or mental duties

If you are unable to supply all of the above information, SSA, with your permission, will contact your employer or anyone else who can.

You will be asked on your Disability and Vocational Reports to thoroughly describe your basic job duties for the job you held the longest in the last 15 years before you stopped working. It is important to provide SSA a full account of your basic responsibilities, including the type of equipment you used and the technical knowledge or skill involved. SSA has a listing of all occupations, each with a detailed job description and a designated nine-digit code number. For example, a security guard job is coded as 372.667-038, and its job description is as follows:

> *Patrols assigned territory to protect persons or property: tours buildings and property of clients, examining doors, windows and gates to assure they are secured. Inspects premises for such irregularities as signs of intrusion and interruption of utility service. Inspects burglar alarm and fire extinguisher sprinkler systems to ascertain they are set to operate. Stands guard during counting of daily cash receipts. Answers alarms and investigates disturbances. Apprehends unauthorized persons. Writes reports of irregularities. May call headquarters at regular intervals, using telephone or portable radio transmitter. May be armed with pistol and be uniformed. May check workers' packages and vehicles entering and leaving premises.*

It is also critical that you break down the physical and mental requirements of your job in your application and convey how your medical restrictions prevent you from doing your past work or any other type of work. A disabled carpenter would not be able to climb, balance, stoop, kneel, crouch, crawl, and reach. A bad case of dermatitis on both hands would make a computer operator, secretary, and typist unable to perform their jobs. If your disability hinders you from doing any of the duties your job requires, indicate this in your application.

You will be asked to describe your "other" jobs in your Vocational Report. Do not repeat the "usual" job listed on your Disability Report. Both of these forms will be discussed further in chapter 7.

PHYSICAL EXERTION REQUIREMENTS

SSA classifies occupations according to their physical demands. Each job falls under one of the following categories:

- *Sedentary*—involves lifting no more than 10 pounds at a time. Although a sedentary job is defined as one that involves sitting, a certain amount of walking and standing is often necessary in carrying out job duties.
- *Light*—involves lifting no more than 20 pounds at a time, with frequent lifting or carrying of objects weighing up to 10 pounds. Even though the weight lifted may be very light, a job in this category requires a good deal of walking or standing. Sitting in such a job usually involves some pushing and pulling of arm or leg controls. If someone can do light work, SSA determines that he/she can also do sedentary work, unless there are additional limiting factors such as loss of fine dexterity or inability to sit for long periods of time.
- *Medium*—involves lifting no more than 50 pounds at a time, with frequent lifting or carrying of objects weighing up to 25 pounds. If someone can do medium work, SSA determines that he/she can also do sedentary and light work.
- *Heavy*—involves lifting no more than 100 pounds at a time, with frequent lifting or carrying of objects weighing up to 50 pounds. If a person can do heavy work, SSA determines that he/she can also do medium, light, and sedentary work.
- *Very heavy work*—involves lifting objects weighing more than 100 pounds, with frequent lifting or carrying of objects weighing more than 50 pounds. If a person can do very heavy work, SSA determines that he/she can also do heavy, medium, light, and sedentary work.

An awareness of these classifications should help you understand how SSA determines an individual's inability to work. A person who is incapable of returning to *any* employment cannot even perform sedentary work. Therefore, you must be unable to lift more than 10 pounds and possess at least one of the following:

- Inability to do minimal walking unless with a cane, walker, or other device
- Inability to bend at the waist without pain due to a defect of the hips or spine
- Inability to sit for a prolonged period of time due to pain
- Inability to use upper extremities
- Farsightedness that is not correctable with glasses
- Hearing loss that makes it unfeasible for you to hear normal speech

For example, if you are unable to stand and walk two hours a day, and this can be substantiated by medical evidence, you would be unable to do sedentary work. If you are unable to sit for extended periods (more than one hour), perhaps because of a back disorder or circulation problem of the legs, or if you are unable to bend at the waist or use fine hand movements, you would also be unable to perform the duties of a sedentary job. Other reasons why you might be unable to do sedentary work include a visual disorder that makes you unable to read standard writing, a significant hearing loss (you must be able to hear at least a normal conversational voice), or needing a cane to walk.

When completing your paperwork, be sure to include anything medically substantiated that would prove you cannot work. If you have a breathing disorder (e.g., asthma or emphysema), mention in your paperwork that you cannot work in environments that would aggravate your disorder, including dusty environments.

Chapter 6

SUPPLEMENTAL SECURITY INCOME (SSI)

The medical requirements needed to prove a disability are the same for both SSDI and SSI. However, eligibility for SSI is based on financial need. The basic purpose of the SSI program is to assure a minimum level of income for people who are age 65 or over, blind, or disabled and who do not have sufficient income or resources to maintain a standard of living at the established federal minimum income level. SSI isn't just for adults; monthly checks can also go to blind and disabled children.

ELIGIBILITY

To be eligible for SSI benefits you must meet all of the following requirements:

1. Age 65 or older, blind, or disabled
2. A resident of the United States and one of the following:
   a) A citizen or national of the United States.
   b) An alien lawfully admitted for permanent residency in the United States.
   c) An alien permanently residing in the United States under color of law. This group includes aliens residing in the United States with the knowledge and permission of

the INS and whose departure INS does not contemplate enforcing. It also includes certain aliens who are residents of long duration. It does not include immigrants.
   d) A child of armed-forces personnel living overseas.
3. Not have more income or resources than is permitted

Why You May Be Ineligible to Receive SSI Benefits

Other Benefits

Even if you meet all of the requirements listed above, you will not be eligible to receive SSI benefits if you do not apply for all other benefits for which you may qualify. Other benefits include annuities, pensions, retirement benefits, and disability benefits. Disability benefits include veterans' compensation and pensions, workers' compensation payments, unemployment insurance benefits, and earned-income tax credits. After you submit an application to SSA, it will send you a dated, written notice that informs you of any other benefits for which you may be eligible. If you do not apply for these other benefits, without a good reason, within 30 days from the day you received SSA's notice, you will be ineligible to receive SSI. Good reasons for not applying for other benefits are the following:

- You are incapacitated; or
- It is useless for you to apply, since you were previously denied benefits and the reasons why you were rejected have not changed.

In addition, if you are found to be eligible to receive other benefits after having already been approved for SSI, your SSI benefits will stop and you will have to repay them beginning with the month you received notice from SSA.

Public Institutions

You are also ineligible to receive SSI for any month you are a resident of a public institution. A public institution is operated or controlled by the federal government, a state government, or a political subdivision of a state, such as a city or county. If you are a resident of a public institution but meet all other eligibility requirements, you will not receive any benefits until you are released from the institution. The amount of SSI benefits for the month of your release will be prorated beginning with the date of your release.

You may be eligible for SSI at a reduced rate if the public institution in which you reside is a medical-care facility and Medicaid pays more than 50 percent of the cost of your care. You'll also qualify if you reside for part of a month in a public institution and the other part in a public or private medical-care facility where Medicaid pays more than 50 percent of the cost of your care.

In addition, if you are a resident of a publicly operated community residence that serves no more than 16 residents, you may be eligible for SSI. To be considered a community residence, a facility must provide food and shelter. It also must make available the following services:

- Social services
- Assistance with personal-living activities
- Training in socialization and life skills
- Occasional or incidental medical or remedial care

VOCATIONAL REHABILITATION SERVICES

SSA may find that an individual can be helped by vocational rehabilitation services. These services are available to SSI recipients between the ages of 16 and 64. If you refuse, without a good reason, to accept these services, you will not be eligible to receive SSI. The following are examples of good reasons:

- The services offered are not designed to restore your ability to work.
- You are already in a program that is expected to restore your ability to work.
- You are regularly attending a school, college, university, or vocational/technical program that is designed to restore your ability to work.
- You're physically or mentally unable to participate in the services offered.
- The services offered interfere with a medical program provided to you.

- The services offered require you to be away from home, which would be harmful to the health and welfare of your family.
- You are working, or you will be working within three months.
- You're a member of a recognized church or religious sect which teaches followers to rely on prayer or other spiritual means for the treatment and care of any physical or mental illness and you refuse to accept these services solely because of these teachings.

Alcoholism or Drug Addiction

If you are a medically determined drug addict or alcoholic, you must accept any treatment prescribed by SSA or you will not receive any benefits.

Leaving the United States

You will lose your eligibility to receive SSI for any month during all of which you are outside the United States (including the District of Columbia and the Northern Mariana Islands). If you leave the United States for 30 consecutive days or more, you will not be considered back in the country until you return for 30 consecutive days—and only then will you again be eligible for SSI.

Redetermination

SSI recipients are redetermined periodically to ensure they are still eligible to receive benefits and that the payments are in the proper amount. The length of time between scheduled redeterminations varies depending on the likelihood that a recipient's situation may change in a way that affects his/her eligibility and/or payment amount.

A redetermination may be conducted in person or by mail or telephone. Individuals are asked to provide the same kind of information that was included in their initial applications and other evidence that may have changed, such as their living arrangements and financial status. If you do not answer SSA's queries within 30 days, SSA may determine you are ineligible to receive any more SSI benefits.

REQUIRED INFORMATION

You must report the following to SSA:

- Change of address
- Change in living arrangements
- Change in income for your spouse or parent
- Change in resources
- Change in eligibility for other benefits
- Change in school attendance
- Death of a parent, spouse, or anyone whose earnings affect your monthly award
- Change in marital status
- Medical improvement
- Refusal to accept vocational rehabilitation services
- Refusal to accept treatment for drug addiction or alcoholism, or a discontinuance of such treatment
- Admission to or discharge from a medical facility or public or private institution
- Termination of residency in the United States
- Temporary departure from the United States

You may report any of the above changes in a written notice or by telephone, telegram, or cable. The report must include your name and the name of the person you are reporting (if different), the Social Security number of the person to whom benefits are paid, the event you are reporting, and the date it occurred. A report is considered late if the event was not disclosed within 10 days after the end of the month in which it happened. A penalty deduction from your benefits may be imposed for a late report: $25 for the first penalty period, $50 for the second, $100 for the third and subsequent penalty periods.

PRESUMPTIVE DISABILITY OR PRESUMPTIVE BLINDNESS

If the evidence available reflects a high degree of probability that you are disabled or blind, SSA may pay you benefits before it makes a formal finding, on the basis that you are presumptively disabled or blind. If you meet all other eligibility requirements, you may receive payments for a period not longer than six months. In cases of readily observable severe impairments, SSA will find you presumptively disabled or blind without medical evidence.

Observable severe impairments include the following:

- Amputation of two limbs
- Amputation of a leg at the hip
- Allegation of total deafness
- Allegation of total blindness
- Allegation of bed confinement or immobility unless with the use of a wheelchair, walker, or crutches, due to a longstanding condition (excluding recent accidents and recent surgeries)
- Allegation of a stroke (cerebral vascular accident) and continued marked difficulty in walking or in using hands or arms
- Allegation of cerebral palsy, muscular dystrophy, or muscle atrophy and marked difficulty in walking, speaking, or coordinating hands or arms
- Allegation of diabetes with amputation of a foot
- Allegation of Down's syndrome (Mongolism)
- Allegation of a severe mental deficiency made by another individual filing on behalf of a claimant who is at least age 7

In all other cases, a finding of a presumptive disability or blindness must be based on medical evidence or other information even if it is not sufficient for a formal determination.

EMERGENCY ADVANCE PAYMENTS

Before making a determination on an application, SSA may pay a one-time emergency advance payment to an individual who is presumptively eligible for SSI benefits and who has a financial emergency. A financial emergency is one in which an individual does not have sufficient income or resources to meet an immediate threat to health or safety. The amount of an advance payment cannot exceed the maximum monthly payment for your particular state of residence.

Once an individual is determined to be eligible, the amount of the emergency advance payment is deducted from his/her benefits. If a presumptively eligible person is determined to be ineligible, the emergency advance payment constitutes a recoverable overpayment. The recipient or another person acting on his/her behalf must refund these monies.

Income

Income is anything you receive in cash or in kind that you can use to meet your needs for food, clothing, and shelter. In-kind income is actual food, clothing, or shelter or something besides cash that you can use to obtain food, clothing, or shelter.

The amount of your monthly checks depends on what you own and how much income you have. If you are married, SSA will examine the income of your spouse and the things he/she owns. If you are under 18, SSA may look at the income of your parents and the things they own.

There are two types of income: earned and unearned.

Earned Income

Earned income consists of the following types of payments:

1. Wages—includes salaries, commissions, bonuses, severance pay, and any other special payments received for your employment.
2. Net earnings from self-employment—gross income from any trade or business you operate, minus allowable deductions. Net earnings also include your share of profit or loss in any partnership to which you belong.
3. Refunds of federal income taxes and advance payments by employers made in accordance with the earned-income-credit provisions of the IRS, under the provisions of Section 43 of the IRS Code of 1954.
4. Payments for services provided in a sheltered workshop or work activities center designed to help you become self-supporting.

UNEARNED INCOME

Unearned income consists of the following types of payments:

1. Annuities, pensions, and other periodic payments usually related to prior work or service. Includes private pensions, Social Security benefits, disability benefits, veterans' benefits, workers' compensation, railroad retirement annuities, and unemployment insurance benefits.
2. Alimony and support payments, in cash or in kind.
3. Dividends, interest, and royalties on capital investments, such as stocks, bonds, or savings accounts.
4. Rents you receive for the use of real or personal property such as land, housing, or machinery.
5. Death benefits from the death of another person, except for the amount of such payments you spend on the deceased person's last illness and burial expenses. Last illness and burial expenses include related hospital and medical expenses, funeral, burial plot and interment expenses, and other related costs.
6. Prizes and awards.
7. Gifts and inheritances you receive, which are not a repayment to you for goods or services you provided, and which are not given to you because of a legal obligation on the giver's part.
8. Support and maintenance in kind, such as food, clothing, or shelter furnished to you.

RESOURCES

The amount of a person's resources is used to determine whether he/she is eligible to receive SSI. Resources are categorized as either liquid or nonliquid:

- Liquid resources are those resources that are in the form of cash or that are convertible to cash within 20 working days. The most common types of liquid resources are savings and checking accounts, stocks, bonds, mutual funds, promissory notes, and certain types of life insurance.
- Nonliquid resources are all resources that cannot be converted into cash within 20 working days. They include both real and personal property.

As of January 1992, an eligible California resident with no spouse can have resources worth up to $2,000; a resident with a spouse can have resources worth up to $3,000. Call your local SSA office to find out the maximum amount of resources you can have in your state to be eligible for SSI.

Items that are excluded from resources are the following:

1. An individual's home, regardless of its value. This exclusion applies to a home owned by the individual or the individual's spouse if it is the principal place of residence. A home includes any adjacent land and related buildings on it.
2. Household goods and personal effects of reasonable value. A reasonable value is considered a $2,000 equity. However, in looking at equity value, SSA excludes one wedding ring and one engagement ring, regardless of their value. SSA also excludes required personal items needed for an individual's condition, such as wheelchairs and prosthetic devices.
3. One automobile, to the extent its value does not exceed the amount set by your state SSA office.
4. Property of a trade or business that is essential to the means of self-support. SSA will exclude up to $6,000 of an individual's equity in income-producing property if it produces a net annual income to the individual of at least 6 percent of the excluded equity. If the equity in such property is greater than $6,000, SSA counts only the amount in excess of $6,000 toward the allowable-resource limit.
5. Nonbusiness property that is essential to the means of self-support if it is used to produce goods or services necessary for an individual's daily activities.
6. Resources of a blind or disabled individual that are necessary to fulfill an approved plan for achieving self-support.
7. Stock in regional or village corporations held by a native of Alaska during the 20-year period in which the stock is inalienable pursuant to the Alaska Native Claims Settlement Act.
8. Life insurance owned by an individual (and spouse, if any).
9. Restricted allotted land owned by an enrolled member of an Indian tribe.
10. Payments or benefits provided under a federal statute other than Title XVI of the Social Security Act, when exclusion is required by such statute.

11. Disaster relief assistance.
12. Burial spaces and burial expenses up to $1,500.
13. Title XVI or Title II retroactive payments.
14. Housing assistance.

Representative Payee

SSA recognizes that every individual has the right to manage his/her own benefits; however, some may be unable to do so. Beneficiaries will be assigned a representative payee, which may be a person or organization, to receive benefits on their behalf if they are one of the following:

- Legally incompetent or mentally incapable of managing benefit payments. A certified copy of the court's findings will be the basis of SSA's determination.
- Physically incapable of managing benefit payments. A statement by a physician or another medical professional based upon a recent examination and his/her knowledge of the beneficiary's present condition will be the basis of SSA's determination.
- A medically determined drug addict or alcoholic.

A beneficiary who is under the age of 18 is generally assigned a representative payee; however, SSA will make an exception if the beneficiary is one of the following:

- A parent and has experience in handling his/her own finances
- Capable of using the benefits to provide for his/her current needs
- Within seven months of turning 18 years old

Selecting a Representative Payee

When selecting a payee, SSA tries to select the person, agency, organization, or institution that will best serve the interest of the beneficiary. In making its selection, SSA considers the following:

- The relationship of the person to the beneficiary
- The amount of interest the person shows in the beneficiary

- Any legal authority the person, agency, organization, or institution has to act on behalf of the beneficiary
- Whether the potential payee has custody of the beneficiary
- Whether the potential payee is in a position to know of and look after the needs of the beneficiary

SSA will take into account any objections an individual might have to a selected representative payee. If a person is dissatisfied with SSA's selection, he/she may request a reconsideration.

A Representative Payee's Obligations

Each representative payee has the responsibility to:

1. Use the payments he/she receives only for the use and benefit of the beneficiary
2. Notify SSA of any event that will affect the amount of benefits the beneficiary receives
3. Submit to SSA, upon its request, a written report accounting for the benefits received
4. Notify SSA of any change in his/her circumstances that would affect the performance of his/her responsibilities

A representative payee is not required to use a beneficiary's payments to pay any bill prior to the first month he/she became a payee. In addition, the payee will be found liable if he/she misuses a beneficiary's benefits.

Once a representative payee is selected, he/she may be asked to supply information that demonstrates both a continuing relationship and a continuing responsibility for the care of the beneficiary. If the payee does not provide the requested information, without a good reason, within a reasonable period of time, SSA may stop issuing payments to the payee.

Accounting for Benefit Payments

Representative payees must keep a record of how all benefit payments are used. Payees may be asked to supply the following information:

- The amount of benefit payments that are available at the beginning of the accounting period.

- How the benefit payments were used.
- How much of the benefit payments were saved and how the savings were invested.
- Where the beneficiary lived during the accounting period.
- The amount of the beneficiary's income from other sources during the accounting period. SSA will ask for information about other funds to enable it to evaluate the use of benefit payments.

WHEN A NEW REPRESENTATIVE PAYEE WILL BE SELECTED

SSA will select a new representative payee if it finds that one or more of the following statements is true of the present payee:

1. The payee has not used the benefit payments on the beneficiary's behalf in accord with established guidelines.
2. The payee has not carried out the other responsibilities described.
3. The payee has died.
4. The payee no longer wishes to be a payee.
5. The payee is unable to manage the benefit payments.
6. The payee fails to cooperate, within a reasonable time, in providing requested information.

Beneficiaries currently assigned a representative payee may request to receive direct payments if they feel that they are mentally and physically able to manage their own benefit payments. Requests for direct payments must be accompanied with the following supporting evidence:

1. A statement from a physician or a medical officer that declares a beneficiary capable of managing his/her own funds.
2. In cases where a beneficiary is found legally incompetent, a certified copy of a court order restoring the beneficiary's rights.
3. Other evidence that establishes the beneficiary's ability to manage or direct benefits.

WORK INCENTIVES

SSI benefits are designed to provide a basic level of support for blind or disabled individuals with restricted earning ability because of their impairments. A number of work incentive provisions have been incorporated into the SSI program so that these individuals may return to work or increase their levels of work activity without losing their SSI disability status. These provisions also protect benefits from being reduced due to any increase in earnings. A few work incentive programs are listed below.

EXTENDED BENEFITS FOR PARTICIPANTS IN VOCATIONAL REHABILITATION PROGRAMS

This provision allows for extended benefits for individuals who recover medically before the end of their vocational rehabilitation program.

IMPAIRMENT-RELATED WORK EXPENSES (IRWE)

The cost of certain impairment-related services and items that a disabled (but not blind) person needs in order to work can be deducted from earnings even if these items and services are also needed for nonwork activities. In calculating IRWE, an amount equal to the cost of certain attendance care services, medical devices, equipment, prostheses, and similar items and services is deductible from earnings. The costs of routine drugs and routine medical services are not deductible unless these drugs and services are necessary to control the disabling condition.

WORK EXPENSES OF THE BLIND

A blind (but not disabled) individual who is receiving both SSI benefits and earned income in any month prior to the attainment of age 65 is entitled to deductible expenses attributable to income earnings. The deductible need not be directly related to the worker's blindness; it need only be an ordinary and necessary work expense. Work expenses include transportation to and from work, meals consumed during work hours, job equipment, licenses, income or Federal Insurance Contributions Act (FICA) taxes, and costs of job training. Expenses for life maintenance (such as life insurance or self-care) are not work-related and are not deductible.

There is no specific dollar limit on the amount that can be deducted under this exclusion. However, the amount must be reasonable and not exceed the individual's earned income in the month. Work expenses are deducted in the month in which the blind individual (or member of a blind couple) makes payment for them.

PLANS FOR ACHIEVING SELF-SUPPORT (PASS)
A plan for achieving self-support allows a disabled or blind person to set aside income and/or resources for a specific goal such as starting a business, getting a degree, or enrolling in a vocational training program. Vocational counselors, social workers, or employers may help an individual with his/her PASS. It is SSA's responsibility to evaluate a PASS and determine its acceptability.

SPECIAL CASH BENEFITS TO DISABLED INDIVIDUALS WHO ENGAGE IN SUBSTANTIAL GAINFUL ACTIVITY
Special SSI cash benefits are provided to individuals whose gross earned income meets the amount designated as the SGA level (currently, earnings over $500 a month). The person must continue to be disabled and meet all other eligibility rules.

To receive the first month of special SSI cash benefits, the person must have been eligible to receive a regular SSI cash payment in a previous month within the current period of eligibility. Then, special benefits may be paid for consecutive months until the individual becomes eligible again under the regular rules or is otherwise ineligible.

EXTENDED MEDICAID ELIGIBILITY FOR PEOPLE WHO WORK
An individual may be eligible for continued Medicaid coverage if he/she continues to work. To qualify for extended Medicaid coverage a person must:

1. Have a disabling condition
2. Need Medicaid in order to work
3. Need Medicaid to afford equivalent medical coverage and publicly funded personal care
4. Meet all non-disability requirements for SSI payment other than earnings
5. Have been eligible to receive a regular SSI cash payment in a previous month within the current period of eligibility

Chapter 7

HOW TO COMPLETE YOUR DISABILITY APPLICATION

This chapter will show you, step by step, how to fill out your disability application. A sample of the application including all questionnaires may be found at the end of the chapter. Before you begin to fill out your application, keep in mind you will be criminally penalized for misrepresenting the facts or for making false statements to obtain Social Security benefits for yourself or for someone else. Also, remember you have to provide enough information to convince SSA you are disabled. Do not allow the space provided to answer the questions to constrain you. If you need more room for answers, use a separate sheet of paper and head it with your name, Social Security number, and the question you are answering. The more thoroughly you can explain your disability, the better SSA will understand your condition.

Make sure to sign and date all forms. Any record, document, or signed statement given to SSA will be kept confidential and will not be disclosed to anyone unless disclosure is specifically required by law. In addition, make copies of all your paperwork; you will need them for your telephone interview.

Begin the application process by calling your local SSA office or SSA's toll-free number, 1-800-772-1213, to request a disability application (you may also request one in person). An SSA representative will ask you a few preliminary questions such as your name, Social

Security number, medical disability, marital status, and current source of income. Within two weeks you will receive an application package that includes an instruction sheet, a disability appointment form, a consultative exam form, a Disability Report, and a Vocational Report.

INSTRUCTION SHEET (EXHIBIT A)

The instruction sheet informs applicants of the types of information and documents they will need to include in their disability application. Your application package must contain the following completed forms:

1. Disability Report, which includes:
   a) Names, addresses, and phone numbers of all medical sources that have treated you
   b) Reasons for visits and treatments received
   c) Treatment dates for visits and inpatient stays
   d) Types of tests you had and when and where they were done
2. Vocational Report, which includes a detailed description of the type of business you worked in during the last 15 years
3. Consultative exam form
4. Disability appointment form

You will also need to submit the following:

- A copy of your Social Security card
- A copy of a certified birth certificate signed by a physician
- A copy of your W-2 form (Wage and Tax Statement) or federal tax return (if self-employed) for the past year
- Dates of any military service
- Dates of all marriages, including a copy of your marriage certificate
- The claim number, effective date, and amount of any other benefit you are or will be expecting to receive because of your disability

DISABILITY APPOINTMENT FORM (EXHIBIT B)

By completing this form, you are requesting SSA to contact you for a telephone interview. Fill in your name, Social Security number, date of birth, the date your disability began, telephone number, and address. If you are married and your spouse is disabled, blind, or age 65 or older, fill in your spouse's name and Social Security number.

The date on the top right-hand corner is used by SSA as the initial date of your claim. SSI applicants must file their paperwork within 60 days from this date; SSDI applicants within six months. In addition, this date will be used by SSA to calculate your monthly awards and retroactive payments (if applicable).

CONSULTATIVE EXAM FORM (EXHIBIT C)

By signing and dating this form, you agree that if a state agency that works with SSA cannot make a decision based on the available medical information, you will attend a requested examination by another doctor(s) at no expense to you. Your signature also acknowledges that if you do not notify the state agency in advance that you cannot keep an appointment, your claim may be denied. Lastly, you agree to notify SSA immediately of any change of address.

DISABILITY REPORT (EXHIBIT D)

You have to prove to SSA that you are blind and/or disabled. This means you must furnish enough medical and other evidence that shows you are disabled and incapable of performing any kind of work. It is wise to make a copy of this form beforehand and use it as a draft copy. Once you complete the form, transfer everything to the original document.

Begin completing this form by filling in your name, Social Security number, and telephone number. In item D briefly explain your impairment.

Part I. Information About Your Condition
Use this part of the form to correlate your disability with your inability to work.

1. Fill in the month, day, and year when your condition first bothered you.
2A. Indicate if you continued to work after the date your condition first bothered you.
2B. If you did continue to work, indicate if your condition caused you to change your job or job duties, hours of work, and attendance.
2C. If you answered yes to any of the items listed in item 2B, explain what the changes in your work circumstances were, the dates they occurred, and how your condition made these changes necessary.
3A. Fill in the month, day, and year when your condition finally made you stop working. Items 1 and 3A do not necessarily have to be the same date, since some people continue to work despite their medical condition.
3B. Explain how your condition now keeps you from working.

Part II. Information About Your Medical Records
Mark the box at the top right-hand corner if you do not have a doctor. Once SSA receives your application, it will make an appointment(s) for you to see an appointed doctor(s) at no cost to you.

4. List the name, address, and telephone number of the doctor who has the latest medical records about your condition. Also indicate how often you see this doctor, the date you first and last saw him/her, the reasons for your visits, and the type of treatment or medicines you received. Make sure that your doctor(s) supplies you with copies of all your medical records so that you can submit them with your initial paperwork. When requesting copies of your medical records, ask your doctor to submit them as soon as possible to avoid any delays in your application process. In addition, ask your doctor if he/she is willing to write a letter that outlines your disability and your inability to work.

How to Complete Your Disability Application 97

- 5A&B. Indicate if you have seen any other doctors since your condition began. If you have, supply the same information that was requested in item 4.
- 6A. Indicate if you were ever hospitalized or treated at a clinic for your disabling condition. If you were, provide the name, address, and phone number of the hospital or clinic. Indicate if you were an inpatient and fill in the dates of your admissions and discharges. If you were an outpatient, fill in the dates of your visits. Describe in detail the reason for your hospitalization or clinic visits as well as the type of treatment or medicines you received. Write "none" if you didn't receive any treatment or medicine.
- 6B. If you have visited another hospital or clinic for your illness, provide the same information here. If you have been in other hospitals or clinics, list the same information in Part VI of the Disability Report. If possible, submit copies of your hospital records with your application.
- 7. Indicate if you have been seen by other agencies for your condition, such as welfare or vocational rehabilitation agencies. If you have, provide the name and address of the agency, your claim number, and the date of visits. Also describe the type of treatment or medicine you received. If you didn't receive any, write "none."
- 8. Indicate if you had any of the tests listed in the last year. If you did, fill in where and when the tests were performed.
- 9. Write down the number of your Medicaid card, if you have one.

Part III. Information About Your Activities

Use this part of the application to correlate your disability with your inability to carry out a variety of activities.

- 10. Indicate if your doctor(s) has told you to reduce or limit your activities. If he/she has, provide the name of the doctor and what he/she has told you about reducing your activities.
- 11. Describe your daily activities for each of the areas listed and indicate how much and how often you do of each.

Part IV. Information About Your Education
As previously mentioned in chapter 5, a lack of education does not mean you are unintelligent, but it might hinder you from working at other jobs.

12. Write down the highest grade level of school you've completed and when.
13. Indicate if you attended a trade or vocational school or had any type of special training. If you did, state the type of trade or vocational school or training, the dates you attended, and how this schooling or training was used in any work you did.

Part V. Information About the Work You Did
14. List all the jobs you have had in the last 15 years before you stopped working, beginning with your usual job. Your usual job refers to the job you held the longest. If you have a sixth-grade education or less, and only did unskilled labor for 35 years or more, list all the jobs you have had since you began to work. Include the dates you worked, the amount of days per week you worked, and the rate of pay you received.
15A. Indicate if you used any kind of machinery, tools, or equipment and technical knowledge or skills in your usual job. Also indicate if your job involved any kind of writing and if you had any supervisory responsibilities.
15B. Provide a full description of your basic job duties. Remember that it is important to break down the physical and mental requirements of your job and convey how your medical restrictions prevent you from doing your past work or any other type of work. Reread the section "Work Experience" in chapter 5 to get a full idea of the type of information to include here. Also, explain all "yes" answers to item 15A by providing a full description of the types of machines, tools, or equipment you used; the technical knowledge or skills involved; the type of writing you did; and the number of people you supervised and the extent of your supervision.
15C. Describe the amount and kind of physical activity involved during a typical day in your usual job. When circling the number of hours you spent walking, standing, and sitting, be sure that the hours total up to an 8-hour working day. For

instance, if you circled 8 hours for each activity you would in essence be saying that you worked a 24-hour working day.

When filling out the disability application for children, show how the disability limits the child's ability to perform age-related activities such as bathing and dressing him/herself. Also mention if the child has a short attention span, problems with basic language skills, and behavioral problems. If IQ tests have been performed, be sure to get copies to include with the application.

Part VI. Remarks

Use this section for additional space to answer any previous questions or to provide any more remarks that may support your disability claim. Also, state in this section if your doctor told you that your disability will last for a certain length of time and that you will eventually be able to return to work.

Once you have entirely completed the Disability Report, sign and date the form. Witnesses are required only if the form is marked "X". If the form is marked "X", two witnesses who know the claimant must sign and date the form as well as provide their addresses.

Vocational Report (Exhibit E)

This report supplements the Disability Report by requesting additional information about your past work experience. Begin completing the form by filling in your name, Social Security number, and telephone number.

Part I. Information About Your Work History

List all the jobs you have had in the last 15 years before you stopped working, beginning with your usual job. Your usual job refers to the job you held the longest. If you have a sixth-grade education or less, and only did unskilled labor for 35 years or more, list all the jobs you have had since you began to work. If you have already given information about your usual job on the Disability Report, begin with your *other* jobs. Do *not* duplicate the job you described in the Disability Report. Include the dates you worked, the amount of days per week you worked, and the rate of pay you received.

Part II. Information About Your Job Duties

Part II provides four pages for you to supply information about four jobs that you listed in Part I. Begin each page by stating your job title. Indicate if you used any kind of machinery, tools, or equipment and technical knowledge or skills in your usual job. Also indicate if your job involved any kind of writing and if you had any supervisory responsibilities. In item *B* provide a full description of your basic job duties. Also, explain all "yes" answers in item *A* by providing a full description of the types of machines, tools, or equipment you used; the technical knowledge or skills involved; the type of writing you did; and the number of people you supervised and the extent of your supervision.

Describe in item *C* the amount and kind of physical activity involved during a typical day in the job you held the longest. Again, when circling the number of hours you spent walking, standing, and sitting, be sure that the hours total up to an eight-hour working day. If you had more than four jobs in the last 15 years, make copies of Part II and add them to your application.

Part III. Remarks

Use this section for additional space to answer any previous question or to provide any more remarks that may support your disability claim. In addition, state in this section if your doctor has told you that your disability will last for a certain length of time and that you will eventually be able to return to work.

Once you have entirely completed the Vocational Report, sign and date the form. Witnesses are required only if the form is marked "X". If the form is marked "X", two witnesses who know the claimant must sign and date the form as well as provide their addresses.

Seizure Questionnaire (Exhibit F)

SSA sends this questionnaire to claimants who suffer from seizures. Make sure to be as thorough as possible when completing this form; refer to the sections on seizures in chapters 3 and 4. In item 5 provide the names, addresses, and phone numbers of people who have observed you having a seizure. The more witnesses you provide, the better your claim will be substantiated.

CHEST PAIN QUESTIONNAIRE (EXHIBIT G)

SSA sends this questionnaire to claimants who have a history of chest pain. Once again, be as thorough as possible when completing this form.

DAILY ACTIVITIES QUESTIONNAIRE (CLAIMANT/THIRD PARTY) (EXHIBIT H)

If SSA determines that it needs more information about your disability, it will send you a Daily Activities Questionnaire to complete. Be as explicit as possible when answering the questions; make sure to convey to SSA any problems you have carrying out your daily activities and any problems that have developed as a result of your medical condition. Note that at the end of the report two referrals are requested; SSA will send them a questionnaire to complete as well. SSA uses a third party to confirm any of the physical or mental restrictions you claim. If the third party does not confirm your claims, SSA will deny your application for disability benefits.

If you did not receive a Daily Activities Questionnaire when you initially applied and your claim was denied, request one now. By reviewing the Daily Activities Questionnaire, you will have a better understanding of how SSA evaluates your disability, which will help you to better prepare your initial or appeals paperwork.

COVER LETTER

Once you complete the entire disability application, write a cover letter to enclose with it. The cover letter should summarize the contents of your application and serve as a checklist for you. There is a sample on the following page.

>
> Susan Jones
> 200 Main St.
> Baltimore, MD 21200
>
> March 1, 1995
>
> SS#: 545-26-2431
>
> Social Security Administration
> 2000 Oak St.
> Los Angeles, CA 90210
>
> Gentlemen:
>
> Enclosed please find the following:
>
> 1. Disability appointment form
> 2. Signed and dated Consultative Exam Statement
> 3. Signed and dated Disability Report
> 4. Signed and dated Vocational Report
> 5. Seizure Questionnaire (if applicable)
> 6. Daily Activities Questionnaire (if applicable)
> 7. Copy of Social Security Card
> 8. Copy of certified birth certificate signed by a physician
> 9. Copy of W-2 Form
> 10. Dates and rank of military service (if applicable)
> 11. Dates of marriage(s) and divorce(s), and a copy of marriage certificate(s) (if applicable)
> 12. (List here the name(s) of each doctor you mentioned in your application)
> 13. Letter(s) from Dr.(s)_____
> 14. Chest Pain Questionnaire (if applicable)
>
> Sincerely,
>
> Susan Jones

Telephone Interview

SSA will notify you of the date and time of your telephone interview about one month after you submit your application. You must be available on the assigned date and time of your interview; if you miss the telephone call, your claim may be denied. Make sure that you have a copy of your complete application in front of you during the interview; the SSA representative will ask you some questions about it. It is important to be both cooperative and polite to the representative. The following are some questions you may be asked during your telephone interview:

1. What are your current name and name at birth (if different)?
2. What is your Social Security number?
3. What are your date and place of birth?
4. What is your disabling condition?
5. Is your condition work related?
6. When did you become unable to work because of your disability?
7. Are you still disabled?
8. Have you filed for disability benefits before? When?
9. Were you ever in the military? (Give dates of service.)
10. Have you filed for any other public disability benefits?
11. Are you entitled to or do you expect to become entitled to a pension?
12. Did you have wages or self-employment covered under Social Security from 1978 through last year?
13. Have you worked for a government or state agency?
14. Were you self-employed this year and last year?
15. How much were your total earnings last year?
16. Did you receive any money from an employer(s) during or after the time you were unable to work because of your disability?
17. Do you expect to receive any additional money from an employer(s), such as sick pay or vacation pay?
18. Have you ever been married? If yes, to whom, when, and where? To whom are you currently married? When and where were you married?
19. Have you or your spouse worked in the railroad industry?
20. What are the ages and names of your children? Are they disabled?
21. Do you have a parent who is dependent on you?
22. Will you assist SSA in getting medical evidence, if needed? (Make sure to answer yes.)

23. Will you authorize SSA to obtain copies of your medical files? (Make sure to answer yes.)
24. If any of your circumstances change, will you notify SSA? (Make sure to answer yes.)
25. Do you own a car? (Note: you cannot have a car worth more than $4,500.)
26. Do you have a bank account?
27. Do you have any money? (Note: In California individuals cannot have more than $2,000; married couples cannot have more than $3,000. Check with your local SSA office on what the limits are. If you have more than the limit, you will not be able to apply for disability benefits and the SSA representative will terminate your phone interview.)
28. Do you take any medications? What are they?
29. Do you have a burial plot?
30. Do you own insurance policies, income-producing property, vehicles, stocks or bonds, or other items that can be turned into cash? Do you have a savings or checking account?
31. Do you have any income such as state disability benefits, unemployment benefits, a pension, or self-employment income?
32. Are you receiving food stamps?
33. Do you need assistance in your personal care?
34. Do you have adequate cooking and food storage facilities available to you?

About one week after your telephone interview, you will receive a computer printout that summarizes everything that was discussed. Sign and date the printout and return it immediately to SSA. Also make sure to keep a copy for your files. Once it receives the printout, SSA will send you a form notifying you of the date a decision will be made on your claim. However, before a decision is made you will probably be asked to see another doctor(s).

While waiting for a determination to be made on your case, make entries in your daily diary concerning any doctor appointments you attend, your medical condition, and any medication you are taking. If your case is denied, a record of this information will help you in the appeals process.

After SSA makes a determination on your case, you will have 60 days from the date of the decision letter to make a reconsideration appeal; otherwise, the determination is binding.

EXHIBIT A

Disability Applications

DISABILITY APPLICATIONS

<u>WHEN YOU RETURN THE ATTACHED FORMS "COMPLETED" WE WILL SCHEDULE YOU FOR AN APPOINTMENT</u>

Disability applications take longer to process than other applications for Social Security benefits. You can shorten the time it takes to complete your claim if you have the following information:

<u>PLEASE COMPLETE:</u>

1. The Disability Report (SSA-3368) must be completed. Special attention is needed for the following for each medical source that has treated you.

    * <u>COMPLETE NAMES</u> for all doctors and hospitals.

    * COMPLETE ADDRESSES AND PHONE NUMBERS for all doctors and hospitals, <u>include zip codes.</u>

    * PATIENT OR CLINIC NUMBERS for all hospitals.

    * REASONS FOR THE VISITS and TREATMENTS RECEIVED.

    * TREATMENT DATES for visits and inpatient stays.

    * TYPES OF TESTS you had, as well as WHEN and WHERE done.

2. The Work History Report (SSA-3369) must be completed. Show the job title and type of business you worked in during the last 15 years.

<u>PLEASE HAVE AVAILABLE</u>

1. Your Social Security number and birth certificate.

2. A copy of your W-2 Form (Wage and Tax Statement), or if you are self-employed, your Federal tax return for the past year.

3. Dates of any military service.

4. Dates of all marriages, current and prior.

5. The claim number, effective date and amount of any other benefit you receive (or expect to receive) because of your disability.

FORMS TO RETURN
- DISABILITY REPORT (SSA-3368)
- WORK HISTORY REPORT (SSA-3369)
- CONSULTATIVE EXAM STATEMENT
- DISABILITY APPOINTMENT SHEET

EXHIBIT B

Disability Appointment

DATE:_____

SR:_____

DISABILITY APPOINTMENT

TO: SOCIAL SECURITY

I WISH TO HAVE AN APPOINTMENT WITH A CLAIMS REPRESENTATIVE TO DISCUSS DISABILITY BENEFITS UNDER SOCIAL SECURITY.

MY NAME IS: _____

MY SOCIAL SECURITY NUMBER IS: _____

MY DATE OF BIRTH IS: _____

MY DISABILITY STARTED ON: _____

MY TELEPHONE NUMBER IS: _____

MY ADDRESS IS: _____

_____

_____

If you are married and live with your spouse, is your spouse disabled, blind, or age 65 or older? If yes:

Spouse's name: _____

Spouse's SS Number: _____

SUPPLEMENTAL SECURITY INCOME (SSI)—The date of this inquiry may be used as your filing date only if we receive a signed application within "SIXTY DAYS" of the date of this notice. If you do not file by this date, you may lose payments because of the limitation of formal applications for Supplemental Security Income.

SOCIAL SECURITY DISABILITY BENEFITS—If you want a formal determination for these benefits, you must file an application within "SIX MONTHS" of the date of this form. If you file within six months of the date of this form, we will use that date as the filing date of your application. If you do not file an application within six months of the date of this form, you may lose benefits because of the six-month limit on retroactivity.

EXHIBIT C

Importance of Keeping a Medical Appointment

IMPORTANCE OF KEEPING A MEDICAL
APPOINTMENT

_____   _____
Claim Number   Name of Number Holder

                                _____
                                Name of Person Making
                                Statement, if Different

It has been explained to me that a decision on my disability application(s) will be made by a State Agency which works with the Social Security Administration. In California, the name of the agency is the Department of Social Services, Division of Disability Evaluation, Fresno, CA. The State Agency asks for medical evidence from my doctors and hospitals. If the State Agency cannot make a decision based on the information from my doctors and hospitals, it may request that I be examined by another doctor(s) at no expense to me. I have been told that:

1. I should go ahead with any medical examination or tests I have already planned, since it is not certain the State Agency will ask me to be examined, and since this may speed up my claim(s).

2. It is my responsibility to cooperate fully with the State Agency if it contacts me by letter or telephone regarding a medical appointment for an examination.

3. If I cannot keep an appointment, I agree to notify the State Agency immediately.

4. If I break an appointment, without telling the State Agency before the appointment, my claim may be denied.

5. If I have filed more than one disability application with Social Security, one claim may be denied, but I still could receive benefits under the other claim, so that I must continue to cooperate with the State Agency.

6. If I change my address, I must notify Social Security immediately.

_____
Signature

_____
Date

EXHIBIT D

Disability Report

DEPARTMENT OF HEALTH AND HUMAN SERVICES
Social Security Administration

Form Approved
OMB No. 0960-0141

DISABILITY REPORT

PLEASE PRINT, TYPE, OR WRITE CLEARLY AND ANSWER ALL ITEMS TO THE BEST OF YOUR ABILITY. If you are filing on behalf of someone else, enter his or her name and social security number in the space provided and answer all questions. COMPLETE ANSWERS WILL AID IN PROCESSING THE CLAIM.

PRIVACY ACT/PAPERWORK REDUCTION ACT NOTICE: The Social Security Administration is authorized to collect the information on this form under sections 205(a), 223(d) and 1633(a) of the Social Security Act. The information on this form is needed by Social Security to make a decision on your claim. While giving us the information on this form is voluntary, failure to provide all or part of the requested information could prevent an accurate or timely decision on your claim and could result in the loss of benefits. Although the information you furnish on this form is almost never used for any purpose other than making a determination on your disability claim, such information may be disclosed by the Social Security Administration as follows: (1) To enable a third party or agency to assist Social Security in establishing rights to Social Security benefits and/or coverage; (2) to comply with Federal laws requiring the release of information from Social Security records (e.g., to the General Accounting Office and the Veterans Administration); and (3) to facilitate statistical research and audit activities necessary to assure the integrity and improvement of the Social Security programs (e.g., to the Bureau of the Census and private concerns under contract to Social Security). These and other reasons why information about you may be used or given out are explained in the Federal Register. If you would like more information about this, any Social Security office can assist you.

A. NAME OF CLAIMANT	B. SOCIAL SECURITY NUMBER	C. TELEPHONE NUMBER where you can be reached (include area code)
	___ ___ ___ / ___ ___ / ___ ___ ___ ___	

D. WHAT IS YOUR DISABLING CONDITION? *(Briefly explain the injury or illness that stops you from working.)*

PART I — INFORMATION ABOUT YOUR CONDITION

1. When did your condition first bother you:	MONTH	DAY	YEAR

2A. Did you work after the date shown in item 1? *(If "no", go on to items 3A and 3B.)*	☐ YES ☐ NO

2B. If you did work since the date in item 1, did your condition cause you to change —

Your job or job duties?	☐ YES ☐ NO
Your hours of work?	☐ YES ☐ NO
Your attendance?	☐ YES ☐ NO
Anything else about your work?	☐ YES ☐ NO

(If you answered "no" to **all** of these, go to items 3A and 3B.)

2C. If you answered "yes" to **any** item in 2B, explain below what the changes in your work circumstances were, the dates they occurred, and how your condition made these changes necessary.

3A. When did your condition finally make you stop working?	MONTH	DAY	YEAR

3B. Explain how your condition now keeps you from working.

Form SSA-3368-BK (1-89)

How to Complete Your Disability Application 109

PART II — INFORMATION ABOUT YOUR MEDICAL RECORDS		
4. List the name, address and telephone number of the doctor who has the latest medical records about your disabling condition.		If you have **no** doctor check ☐

NAME	ADDRESS
TELEPHONE NUMBER (include area code)	

HOW OFTEN DO YOU SEE THIS DOCTOR?	DATE YOU **FIRST** SAW THIS DOCTOR	DATE YOU **LAST** SAW THIS DOCTOR

REASONS FOR VISITS (show illness or injury for which you had an examination or treatment)

TYPE OF TREATMENT OR MEDICINES RECEIVED (such as surgery, chemotherapy, radiation, and the medicines you take for your illness or injury, if known. If no treatment or medicines, show "NONE".)

5A. Have you seen any other doctors since your disabling condition began? If "yes", show the following:		☐ YES ☐ NO

NAME	ADDRESS
TELEPHONE NUMBER (include area code)	

HOW OFTEN DO YOU SEE THIS DOCTOR?	DATE YOU **FIRST** SAW THIS DOCTOR	DATE YOU **LAST** SAW THIS DOCTOR

REASONS FOR VISITS (show illness or injury for which you had an examination or treatment)

TYPE OF TREATMENT OR MEDICINES RECEIVED (such as surgery, chemotherapy, radiation, and the medicines you take for your illness or injury, if known. If no treatment or medicines, show "NONE".)

5B. Identify below any other doctor you have seen since your illness or injury began.

NAME	ADDRESS
TELEPHONE NUMBER (include area code)	

HOW OFTEN DO YOU SEE THIS DOCTOR?	DATE YOU **FIRST** SAW THIS DOCTOR	DATE YOU **LAST** SAW THIS DOCTOR

REASONS FOR VISITS (show illness or injury for which you had an examination or treatment.)

TYPE OF TREATMENT OR MEDICINES RECEIVED (such as surgery, chemotherapy, radiation, and the medicines you take for your illness or injury, if known. If no treatment or medicines, show "NONE".)

Form SSA-3368-BK (1-89)

6A. Have you been hospitalized or treated at a clinic for your disabling condition?
If "yes", show the following: ☐ YES ☐ NO

NAME OF HOSPITAL OR CLINIC

ADDRESS

PATIENT OR CLINIC NUMBER

WERE YOU AN INPATIENT? (stayed at least overnight?)
☐ YES ☐ NO (If "yes", show:)

DATES OF ADMISSIONS	DATES OF DISCHARGES

WERE YOU AN OUTPATIENT?
☐ YES ☐ NO (If "yes", show:)

DATES OF VISITS

REASON FOR HOSPITALIZATION OR CLINIC VISITS *(show illness or injury for which you had an examination or treatment.)*

TYPE OF TREATMENT OR MEDICINES RECEIVED (such as surgery, chemotherapy, radiation, and the medicines you take for your illness or injury, if known. If no treatment or medicines, show "NONE".)

6B. If you have been in other hospital or clinic for your illness or injury, identify it below.

NAME OF HOSPITAL OR CLINIC

ADDRESS

PATIENT OR CLINIC NUMBER

WERE YOU AN INPATIENT? (stayed at least overnight?)
☐ YES ☐ NO (If "yes", show:)

DATES OF ADMISSIONS	DATES OF DISCHARGES

WERE YOU AN OUTPATIENT?
☐ YES ☐ NO (If "yes", show:)

DATES OF VISITS

REASON FOR HOSPITALIZATION OR CLINIC VISITS *(show illness or injury for which you had an examination or treatment.)*

TYPE OF TREATMENT OR MEDICINES RECEIVED (such as surgery, chemotherapy, radiation, and the medicines you take for your illness or injury, if known. If no treatment or medicines, show "NONE".)

If you have been in other hospitals or clinics for your illness or injury, list the names, addresses, patient or clinic numbers, dates and reasons for hospitalization or clinic visits in Part VI.

7. Have you been seen by other agencies for your disabling condition?
(VA, Workmen's Compensation, Vocational Rehabilitation, Welfare, etc.)
(If "yes," show the following:) ☐ YES ☐ NO

NAME OF AGENCY

ADDRESS

YOUR CLAIM NUMBER

DATE OF VISITS

TYPE OF TREATMENT, EXAMINATION OR MEDICINES RECEIVED (such as surgery, chemotherapy, radiation, and the medicines you take for your illness or injury, if known. If no treatment or medicines, show "NONE".)

If more space is needed, list the other agencies, their addresses, your claim numbers, dates, and treatment received in Part VI.

Form SSA-3368-BK (1-89)

How to Complete Your Disability Application 111

8. Have you had any of the following tests in the last year?

TEST	CHECK APPROPRIATE BLOCK OR BLOCKS	IF "YES" SHOW	
		WHERE DONE	WHEN DONE
Electrocardiogram	☐ YES ☐ NO		
Chest X-Ray	☐ YES ☐ NO		
Other X-Ray (name body part here)	☐ YES ☐ NO		
Breathing Tests	☐ YES ☐ NO		
Blood Tests	☐ YES ☐ NO		
Other (Specify)	☐ YES ☐ NO		

9. If you have a medicaid card, what is your number (some hospitals and clinics file your records by your medicaid number.)

PART III — INFORMATION ABOUT YOUR ACTIVITIES

10. Has your doctor told you to cut back or limit your activities in any way? ☐ YES ☐ NO
If "yes", give the name of the doctor below and tell what he or she told you about cutting back or limiting your activities.

11. Describe your daily activities in the following areas and state what and how much you do of each and how often you do it:
   - Household maintenance (including cooking, cleaning, shopping, and odd jobs around the house as well as any other similar activities):

   - Recreational activities and hobbies (hunting, fishing, bowling, hiking, musical instruments, etc.):

   - Social contacts (visits with friends, relatives, neighbors):

   - Other (drive car, motorcycle, ride bus, etc.)

Form SSA-3368-BK (1-89)

112 How You Can Apply for Social Security Disability Benefits

PART IV — INFORMATION ABOUT YOUR EDUCATION

12. What is the highest grade of school that you completed and when?

13. Have you gone to trade or vocational school or had any type of special training? *If "yes", show:*   ☐ YES ☐ NO

- The type of trade or vocational school or training:
- Approximate dates you attended:
- How this schooling or training was used in any work you did:

PART V — INFORMATION ABOUT THE WORK YOU DID

14. List all jobs you have had in the last 15 years before you stopped working, beginning with your usual job. Normally, this will be the kind of work you did the longest. (If you have a 6th grade education or less, AND did only heavy unskilled labor for 35 years or more, list all of the jobs you have had since you began to work. If you need more space, use Part VI.)

JOB TITLE (Be sure to begin with your usual job)	TYPE OF BUSINESS	DATES WORKED (Month and Year)		DAYS PER WEEK	RATE OF PAY (Per hour, day, week, month or year)
		FROM	TO		

15A. Provide the following information for your usual job shown in item 14, line 1.

In your job did you:
- Use machines, tools, or equipment of any kind?   ☐ Yes ☐ No
- Use technical knowledge or skills?   ☐ Yes ☐ No
- Do any writing, complete reports, or perform similar duties?   ☐ Yes ☐ No
- Have supervisory responsibilities?   ☐ Yes ☐ No

15B. Describe your basic duties (explain what you did and how you did it) below. Also, explain all "Yes" answers by giving a FULL DESCRIPTION of: the types of machines, tools, or equipment you used and the exact operation you performed; the technical knowledge or skills involved; the type of writing you did, and the nature of any reports; and the number of people you supervised and the extent of your supervision:

Form SSA-3368-BK (1-89)

15C. Describe the kind and amount of physical activity this job involved during typical day in terms of:

- **Walking** (circle the number of hours a day spent walking) — 0 1 2 3 4 5 6 7 8
- **Standing** (circle the number of hours a day spent standing) — 0 1 2 3 4 5 6 7 8
- **Sitting** (circle the number of hours a day spent sitting) — 0 1 2 3 4 5 6 7 8
- **Bending** (circle how often a day you had to bend) — Never · Occasionally · Frequently · Constantly
- **Reaching** (circle how often a day you had to reach) — Never · Occasionally · Frequently · Constantly
- **Lifting and Carrying:** Describe below what was lifted, and how far it was carried. Check heaviest weight lifted, and weight frequently lifted and/or carried:

HEAVIEST WEIGHT LIFTED	WEIGHT FREQUENTLY LIFTED/CARRIED
☐ 10 lbs. ☐ 20 lbs. ☐ 50 lbs. ☐ 100 lbs. ☐ Over 100 lbs.	☐ Up to 10 lbs. ☐ Up to 25 lbs. ☐ Up to 50 lbs. ☐ Over 50 lbs.

PART VI — REMARKS

Use this section for additional space to answer any previous questions. Also use this space to give any additional information that you think will be helpful in making a decision in your disability claim, (such as information about other illnesses or injuries not shown in Parts I and II.) Please refer to the previous items by number.

Public reporting burden for this collection of information is estimated to average 30 minutes per response, including the time for reviewing instructions, searching existing data sources, gathering and maintaining the data needed, and completing and reviewing the collection of information. Send comments regarding this burden estimate or any other aspect of this collection of information, including suggestions for reducing this burden to the Social Security Administration ATTN: Reports Clearance Officer, 1-A-21 Operations Bldg., Baltimore, MD 21235 and to the Office of Management and Budget, Paperwork Reduction Project (OMB #0960-0141), Washington, D.C. 20503.

Knowing that anyone making a false statement or representation of a material fact for use in determining a right to payment under the Social Security Act commits a crime punishable under Federal law, I certify that the above statements are true.

NAME (Signature of claimant or person filing on the claimant's behalf)

SIGN HERE ▶ | DATE

Witnesses are required ONLY if this statement has been signed by mark (X) above. If signed by mark (X), two witnesses to the signing who know the person making the statement must sign below, giving their full addresses.

1. Signature of Witness	2. Signature of Witness
Address (Number and street, city, state, and ZIP code)	Address (Number and street, city, state, and ZIP code)

Form SSA-3368-BK (1-89)

114 *How You Can Apply for Social Security Disability Benefits*

EXHIBIT E

Vocational Report

DEPARTMENT OF HEALTH AND HUMAN SERVICES
SOCIAL SECURITY ADMINISTRATION

Form Approved
OMB No. 0960-0141

VOCATIONAL REPORT

This report supplements the Disability Report (Form SSA-3368-F8) by requesting additional information about your past work experience. PLEASE PRINT, TYPE, OR WRITE CLEARLY AND ANSWER ALL ITEMS TO THE BEST OF YOUR ABILITY. If you are filing on behalf of someone else, enter his or her name and social security number in the space provided and answer all questions. COMPLETE ANSWERS WILL AID IN PROCESSING THE CLAIM.

PRIVACY ACT NOTICE: The information requested on this form is authorized by Title 20 CFR 404.1512 and Title 20 CFR 416.912. The information provided will be used in making a decision on your claim. While completion of this form is voluntary, failure to provide all or part of the requested information could prevent an accurate or timely decision on your claim and could result in the loss of some benefits. Information you furnish on this form may be disclosed by the Social Security Administration to another person or governmental agency only with respect to social security programs and to comply with Federal laws requiring the exchange of information between Social Security and another agency.

A. Name of Claimant	B. Social Security Number	C. Telephone number where you can be reached (include area code)

PART I — INFORMATION ABOUT YOUR WORK HISTORY

List all jobs you have had in the last 15 years before you stopped working, beginning with your usual job; normally, this will be the kind of work you did the longest. (If you have a 6th grade education or less, **AND** did only heavy unskilled labor for 35 years or more, list all of the jobs you have had since you began to work. If you need more space, use Part III.) If you have already given information about your usual job on the Form SSA-3368-F8 (Disability Report), begin with your other jobs.

	JOB TITLE (Be sure to begin with your usual job)	TYPE OF BUSINESS	DATES WORKED (Month and Year)		DAYS PER WEEK	RATE OF PAY (Per hour, day, week, month or year)
			FROM	TO		
1						
2						
3						
4						
5						
6						
7						
8						
9						
10						
11						
12						

FORM **SSA-3369-F6** (3-82) DESTROY PRIOR EDITIONS

PART II — INFORMATION ABOUT YOUR JOB DUTIES

Provide the following information (on pages 2-5) for each of the jobs listed in Part I starting with your usual job:

Job Title (from Part I):

A. In your job did you:
- Use machines, tools, or equipment of any kind? ☐ Yes ☐ No
- Use technical knowledge or skills? ☐ Yes ☐ No
- Do any writing, complete reports, or perform similar duties? ☐ Yes ☐ No
- Have supervisory responsibilities? ☐ Yes ☐ No

B. Describe your basic duties (explain what you did and how you did it) below. Also, explain all "Yes" answers by giving a FULL DESCRIPTION of: the types of machines, tools, or equipment you used and the exact operation you performed; the technical knowledge or skills involved; the type of writing you did, and the nature of any reports; and the number of people you supervised and the extent of your supervision;

C. Describe the kind and amount of physical activity this job involved during a typical day in terms of:

- **Walking** (circle the number of hours a day spent walking) — 0 1 2 3 4 5 6 7 8
- **Standing** (circle the number of hours a day spent standing) — 0 1 2 3 4 5 6 7 8
- **Sitting** (circle the number of hours a day spent sitting) — 0 1 2 3 4 5 6 7 8
- **Bending** (circle how often a day you had to bend) — Never · Occasionally · Frequently · Constantly
- **Lifting and Carrying:** Describe what was lifted, and how far it was carried. Check below heaviest weight lifted, and weight frequently lifted and/or carried.

Heaviest weight lifted	Weight frequently lifted/carried
☐ 10 lbs.	☐ Up to 10 lbs.
☐ 20 lbs.	☐ Up to 25 lbs.
☐ 50 lbs.	☐ Up to 50 lbs.
☐ 100 lbs.	☐ Over 50 lbs.
☐ Over 100 lbs.	

FORM SSA-3369-F6 (3-82)

116 How You Can Apply for Social Security Disability Benefits

Job Title (from Part I):

A. In your job did you:
- Use machines, tools, or equipment of any kind? ☐ Yes ☐ No
- Use technical knowledge or skills? ☐ Yes ☐ No
- Do any writing, complete reports, or perform similar duties? ☐ Yes ☐ No
- Have supervisory responsibilities? ☐ Yes ☐ No

B. Describe your basic duties (explain what you did and how you did it) below. Also, explain all "Yes" answers by giving a FULL DESCRIPTION of: the types of machines, tools, or equipment you used and the exact operation you performed; the technical knowledge or skills involved; the type of writing you did, and the nature of any reports; and the number of people you supervised and the extent of your supervision:

C. Describe the kind and amount of physical activity this job involved during a typical day in terms of:

- **Walking** (circle the number of hours a day spent walking) — 0 1 2 3 4 5 6 7 8
- **Standing** (circle the number of hours a day spent standing) — 0 1 2 3 4 5 6 7 8
- **Sitting** (circle the number of hours a day spent sitting) — 0 1 2 3 4 5 6 7 8
- **Bending** (circle how often a day you had to bend) — Never · Occasionally · Frequently · Constantly
- **Lifting and Carrying:** Describe what was lifted, and how far it was carried. Check below heaviest weight lifted, and weight frequently lifted and/or carried.

Heaviest weight lifted	Weight frequently lifted/carried
☐ 10 lbs.	☐ Up to 10 lbs.
☐ 20 lbs.	☐ Up to 25 lbs.
☐ 50 lbs.	☐ Up to 50 lbs.
☐ 100 lbs.	☐ Over 50 lbs.
☐ Over 100 lbs.	

FORM **SSA-3369-F6** (3-82)

How to Complete Your Disability Application 117

Job Title (from Part I):

A. In your job did you:
- Use machines, tools, or equipment of any kind? ☐ Yes ☐ No
- Use technical knowledge or skills? ☐ Yes ☐ No
- Do any writing, complete reports, or perform similar duties? ☐ Yes ☐ No
- Have supervisory responsibilities? ☐ Yes ☐ No

B. Describe your basic duties (explain what you did and how you did it) below. Also, explain all "Yes" answers by giving a FULL DESCRIPTION of: the types of machines, tools, or equipment you used and the exact operation you performed; the technical knowledge or skills involved; the type of writing you did, and the nature of any reports; and the number of people you supervised and the extent of your supervision:

C. Describe the kind and amount of physical activity this job involved during a typical day in terms of:

- **Walking** (circle the number of hours a day spent walking) — 0 1 2 3 4 5 6 7 8
- **Standing** (circle the number of hours a day spent standing) — 0 1 2 3 4 5 6 7 8
- **Sitting** (circle the number of hours a day spent sitting) — 0 1 2 3 4 5 6 7 8
- **Bending** (circle how often a day you had to bend) — Never · Occasionally · Frequently · Constantly
- **Lifting and Carrying:** Describe what was lifted, and how far it was carried. Check below heaviest weight lifted, and weight frequently lifted and/or carried.

Heaviest weight lifted	Weight frequently lifted/carried
☐ 10 lbs.	☐ Up to 10 lbs.
☐ 20 lbs.	☐ Up to 25 lbs.
☐ 50 lbs.	☐ Up to 50 lbs.
☐ 100 lbs.	☐ Over 50 lbs.
☐ Over 100 lbs.	

FORM SSA-3369-F6 (3-82)

118 How You Can Apply for Social Security Disability Benefits

Job Title (from Part I):

A. In your job did you:
- Use machines, tools, or equipment of any kind? ☐ Yes ☐ No
- Use technical knowledge or skills? ☐ Yes ☐ No
- Do any writing, complete reports, or perform similar duties? ☐ Yes ☐ No
- Have supervisory responsibilities? ☐ Yes ☐ No

B. Describe your basic duties (explain what you did and how you did it) below. Also, explain all "Yes" answers by giving a FULL DESCRIPTION of: the types of machines, tools, or equipment you used and the exact operation you performed; the technical knowledge or skills involved; the type of writing you did, and the nature of any reports; and the number of people you supervised and the extent of your supervision:

C. Describe the kind and amount of physical activity this job involved during a typical day in terms of:

- **Walking** (circle the number of hours a day spent walking) — 0 1 2 3 4 5 6 7 8
- **Standing** (circle the number of hours a day spent standing) — 0 1 2 3 4 5 6 7 8
- **Sitting** (circle the number of hours a day spent sitting) — 0 1 2 3 4 5 6 7 8
- **Bending** (circle how often a day you had to bend) — Never · Occasionally · Frequently · Constantly
- **Lifting and Carrying:** Describe what was lifted, and how far it was carried. Check below heaviest weight lifted, and weight frequently lifted and/or carried.

Heaviest weight lifted	Weight frequently lifted/carried
☐ 10 lbs.	☐ Up to 10 lbs.
☐ 20 lbs.	☐ Up to 25 lbs.
☐ 50 lbs.	☐ Up to 50 lbs.
☐ 100 lbs.	☐ Over 50 lbs.
☐ Over 100 lbs.	

IF YOU NEED ADDITIONAL SPACE TO PROVIDE INFORMATION ABOUT OTHER JOBS LISTED IN PART I OF THIS FORM, USE PART III OR ASK THE SOCIAL SECURITY OFFICE FOR ADDITIONAL COPIES OF THIS FORM.

FORM SSA-3369-F6 (3-82)

PART III — REMARKS

Use this section for any other information you may want to give about your work history, or to provide any other remarks you may want to make to support your disability claim:

_____

_____

_____   _____

_____

_____

_____

_____   _____

_____

_____

_____

_____

_____

(If you need more space, use separate sheets of paper.)

Knowing that anyone making a false statement or representation of a material fact for use in determining a right to payment under the Social Security Act commits a crime punishable under Federal law, I certify that the above statements are true.

NAME (Signature of Claimant or Person Filing on the Claimant's Behalf)

SIGN HERE ▶   DATE

Witnesses are required ONLY if this statement has been signed by mark (X) above. If signed by mark (X), two witnesses to the signing who know the person making the statement must sign below, giving their full addresses.

1. Signature of Witness	2. Signature of Witness
Address (Number and street, city, state, and ZIP code)	Address (Number and street, city, state, and ZIP code)

Do not write below this line

SSA-3369-F6 taken by: ☐ PERSONAL INTERVIEW ☐ TELEPHONE ☐ MAIL	FORM SUPPLEMENTED: If "Yes," by ☐ PERSONAL INTERVIEW	☐ YES ☐ NO ☐ TELEPHONE ☐ MAIL
SIGNATURE OF INTERVIEWER OR REVIEWER	TITLE (also check office) ☐ DDS ☐ DO ☐ BO	DATE

FORM SSA-3369-F6 (3-82)

EXHIBIT F

Seizure Questionnaire

State of California - Health and Welfare Agency
DEPARTMENT OF SOCIAL SERVICES - DISABILITY EVALUATION DIVISION
P.O. Box 1072
Fresno, CA. 93714

Re:_____

Please complete the following questionnaire regarding the above person's seizure activity. If additional space is needed, please use back of form. Please return this form to us within 10 days. Thank You.

1. How often do seizures occur?	When was the last one?	When was the last one before that?

2. Please describe a typical seizure.

3. What happens when the seizure is over?

4. What medication is being taken for seizures?

Describe any side effects.

5. Please provide the name, address, and phone number of people who have observed a seizure.

6. When and where was your last EEG performed?

Form Completed by: _____ Date: _____

Disability Evaluation Analyst: _____ Phone: (209) 287-_____

Fresno-Line 47(12/92) SEIZURE QUESTIONNAIRE

EXHIBIT G

Chest Pain Questionnaire

TERRY E. BRANSTAD, GOVERNOR

DEPARTMENT OF EDUCATION
AL RAMIREZ, Ed.D., DIRECTOR

CHEST PAIN QUESTIONNAIRE

1. What does the pain feel like? Steady? Pressure? Sharp? Burning?

2. Where is it located? Under breastbone (necktie area)? Left side? Other? Does it sometimes radiate to other areas?

3. How long does it usually last? (A second or two? 3-4 minutes? 5-10 minutes? 20-30 minutes? Hours?)

4. What brings it on? (give examples). How soon will it bring it on?

   Stress?

   Exertion?

   Deep breath? Touching sore spot on chest?

   Use of arms? If so, which one?

   What position of arm?

   Lying in a certain position?

   Exposure to cold air or a hot day?

   Hurrying?

   Climbing stairs? How many flights?

   A large meal? Being hungry?

   Combination of 2 or more of the above simultaneously?

4407
LYR/RAF

DIVISION OF VOCATIONAL REHABILITATION SERVICES / 510 EAST 12TH / DES MOINES, IOWA 50319

TERRY E. BRANSTAD, GOVERNOR

DEPARTMENT OF EDUCATION
AL RAMIREZ, Ed.D., DIRECTOR

CHEST PAIN QUESTIONNAIRE (continued)

5. How far can you walk without stopping? What makes you stop?

   How long does it take you to walk that far?

6. What is the heaviest work you have done recently?

   Can you lift and carry 10#? 25#? 50#?

7. What relieves the pain, and how quickly in each case?

   Rest

   Nitroglycerine tablet or spray

   Lying down

   Getting up and walking around

   Antacid name?

   Nothing helps, it just goes away.

8. Have you ever had hiatal heria, or difficulty swallowing?

4407
LYR/RAF

DIVISION OF VOCATIONAL REHABILITATION SERVICES / 510 EAST 12TH / DES MOINES, IOWA 50319

How to Complete Your Disability Application 123

TERRY E. BRANSTAD, GOVERNOR

DEPARTMENT OF EDUCATION
AL RAMIREZ, Ed.D., DIRECTOR

CHEST PAIN QUESTIONNAIRE (continued)

9. Has the pain been getting better or worse recently? Explain.

10. Add any comments you wish to more adequately explain your symptoms.

_____   _____
Claimant's Signature   Date

4407
LYR/RAF

DIVISION OF VOCATIONAL REHABILITATION SERVICES / 510 EAST 12TH / DES MOINES, IOWA 50319

124 *How You Can Apply for Social Security Disability Benefits*

EXHIBIT H

Daily Activities Questionnaire

STATE OF CALIFORNIA — HEALTH AND WELFARE AGENCY

DAILY ACTIVITIES QUESTIONNAIRE

APPLICANT NAME	SOCIAL SECURITY NUMBER	DATE

The answers to these questions will help us to determine whether your condition is disabling within the meaning of the law. Please explain your answers wherever possible by giving descriptions and examples. If you need more room for your answers, you may use additional sheets. Your cooperation is appreciated.

GENERAL INFORMATION

1. Where do you currently live?

   ☐ Home ☐ Apartment ☐ Boarding House ☐ Nursing Home ☐ Other

   If other, please explain.

2. With whom do you live?

   ☐ Alone ☐ With Family ☐ With Friends ☐ Board and Care ☐ Other

   If other, please explain.

ACTIVITIES OF DAILY LIVING

1. Please describe what you do on an average day.

2. A. What difficulties, if any, do you have sleeping?

   B. Do you take medication to sleep? If YES, what type and how often?

3. What difficulties, if any, do you have caring for your own personal needs (e.g., grooming, dressing, cleaning, etc.)? Do you require any type of assistance? If YES, please explain.

4. A. Who prepares and cooks your meals?

   B. How often and what type foods do you cook?

DEP 2059 (5/87)

How to Complete Your Disability Application 125

5. A. What shopping do you do? How often?

   B. Does anyone help you with your shopping? If so, what type of help do you need?

6. A. What household chores are you able to do (i.e., cleaning, laundry, maintenance, ironing, etc.)?

   B. Do you need any help completing these chores? If so, please explain.

7. What type of activities or hobbies do you enjoy and spend time on?

8. A. How often do you listen to the radio or watch TV? What types of programs do you listen to or watch? Are you able to remember the programs that you heard or watched?

   B. How often do you read? What do you read (i.e., books, newspapers, magazines)? Are you able to remember what you read?

SOCIAL FUNCTIONING

1. A. How often do you go out of your home?

   B. When you go out, do you:

   ☐ Walk   ☐ Ride the Bus   ☐ Drive a Car   ☐ Other

   Please explain:

   C. Where do you generally go?

   D. What help, if any, do you need to get out?

2. What difficulties, if any, do you have getting along with family, friends, neighbors, co-workers or others? Please explain.

3. A. How often do you visit family or friends, or have them visit you? What do you do during the visits?

   B. How often do you talk to relatives on the telephone?

4. Who is dependent upon you for care (i.e., spouse, children, parents, pets)? What assistance do you give them?

5. What community, church, sports, or social groups do you belong to? Are you active in these groups? How do you participate?

6. What types of activities or hobbies do you do for entertainment?

7. Have your social activities changed since your condition began?

PERSONAL INFORMATION

1. Do you ever have problems concentrating? If so, please give examples.

2. When you begin a task or chore do you ever have trouble finishing the job? If so, please give examples.

3. What type of difficulty, if any, do you have in following written or verbal instructions (i.e., cooking instructions or someone giving directions)?

4. What medications do you take for your condition? Do you take it yourself or does someone give it to you?

How to Complete Your Disability Application 127

5. Please explain how your condition keeps you from working.

6. Have you tried to work after you became ill? If so, what happened?

7. Have you ever lost your job as a result of your condition? Please explain.

GENERAL

We may need further information on your condition. Please list the names, addresses, telephone numbers, and relationship of any friends, relatives, or others (i.e., rehabilitation counselor, social worker, landlord) whom we may contact who know about your medical condition.

1. NAME						RELATIONSHIP
ADDRESS	NUMBER	STREET	CITY	STATE	ZIP CODE	TELEPHONE
2. NAME						RELATIONSHIP
ADDRESS	NUMBER	STREET	CITY	STATE	ZIP CODE	TELEPHONE

If you have worked in the last two years, please list an employer whom we may contact for further information about your condition.

COMPANY NAME						TELEPHONE
ADDRESS	NUMBER	STREET	CITY		STATE	ZIP CODE
SUPERVISOR			DATES EMPLOYED			

Did you need help completing this form?   ☐ YES   ☐ NO

If YES, who assisted you?

NAME						RELATIONSHIP
ADDRESS	NUMBER	STREET	CITY	STATE	ZIP CODE	TELEPHONE
APPLICANT'S SIGNATURE (Please sign and return this form within 10 days in the self-addressed, stamped envelope provided)						DATE
DISABILITY ANALYST SIGNATURE (If information taken over the phone)						DATE

DFA INSTRUCTIONS: If information taken over the telephone, any additional comments or observations may be completed on the opposite side of this page or an SSA-5002, Report of Contact Form.

Chapter 8

You've Been Approved!

If you have been approved to receive disability benefits, you will receive an award letter that fully explains your monthly awards and a booklet that summarizes both your and SSA's responsibilities. One of your obligations is to notify SSA promptly if one of the following events occurs:

- Your condition improves.
- You return to work.
- You increase the amount of your work.
- Your earnings increase.

In addition, your case will be reviewed periodically to verify you are still disabled. If your medical condition is expected to improve, your case may be reviewed within 6 to 18 months from the date your benefits begin; if an improvement is *possible,* your case will be reviewed no sooner than three years; and, if your condition is *not expected* to improve, your case will be reviewed no sooner than seven years.

When Your Disability Benefits Will Cease

You will stop receiving disability benefits if:

1. You work and the earnings you receive are considered to be substantial by SSA. Usually, average earnings of $500 or more per month are considered to be substantial.

2. SSA determines that your medical condition has improved to the point that it can determine you are no longer disabled.
3. You are confined in a jail, prison, or other penal or correctional institution for conviction of a felony. This rule only applies to the prisoner; benefit payments to any other person who is entitled to them on the basis of the prisoner's wages and self-employment income will continue.
4. You refuse without a good reason to accept rehabilitation services available to you under a state plan approved under the Vocational Rehabilitation Act. An individual has good cause for refusing rehabilitation services when:

   a. The individual is a member or adherent of any recognized church or religious sect that teaches its members or adherents to rely solely, in the treatment and care of any physical or mental impairment, on prayer or spiritual means through the application and use of the tenets or teachings of such church or sect; and
   b. The individual's refusal to accept rehabilitation services is due solely to adherence to the teachings or tenets of this church or sect.

Payments

SSDI checks are usually dated and delivered on the third day of the month following the month for which the payment is due. For example, checks for January are delivered on February 3. If the third of the month is a Saturday, Sunday, or federal holiday, checks are dated and delivered on the first day preceding the third day of the month that is not a Saturday, Sunday, or federal holiday. For example, if the third day of the month is a Saturday or Sunday, checks are delivered on the preceding Friday.

SSI checks are usually dated and delivered on the first day of the month for which they are due. However, if the first day of the month falls on a Saturday, Sunday, or federal holiday, checks are dated and delivered on the first day preceding the first day of the month that is not a Saturday, Sunday, or federal holiday.

You will not be able to cash a check any later than one year from when the check was issued. If you pass the one-year time limit, contact SSA immediately so that it can reissue another check for you.

Lost Checks
If you have not received a check within three days after it is usually received or if the check has been stolen, lost, destroyed, or forged, contact SSA immediately. Supply SSA with your Social Security claim number on which the benefits are being paid, the period of payment covered by the missing check(s), and the name and address that would be shown on the check.

Change of Address
A change of address should be reported promptly to SSA in writing and signed by the payee. If a person is unable to sign his/her name, a signature by mark is acceptable. A signature by mark must be witnessed by two individuals who also sign their own names and provide their complete addresses. You may also report a change of address by telephone; however, if there is any doubt about the authenticity of a telephone report, SSA will request written confirmation from the payee. The Social Security claim number and the individual's old address should also be given so that any check already printed can be found and sent to the new address. In addition, your local post office should be notified of the change of address to ensure prompt delivery of checks.

Direct Deposits
A beneficiary may request that payments be directly deposited into an account at a financial institution. A financial institution may be a bank, trust company, savings and loan association, or a federal or state chartered credit union. Direct deposits are particularly helpful for those beneficiaries who have trouble traveling or who are concerned about loss or theft of their checks.

Garnished Checks
Future Social Security disability benefits cannot be assigned. Also, Social Security disability benefits are not subject to levy, garnishment, or attachment except in very restricted circumstances, such as by a court order for the collection of child support or alimony or by the Internal Revenue Service for unpaid federal taxes.

FORM 1099 (SOCIAL SECURITY BENEFIT STATEMENT)
At the end of the year you will receive a Form 1099, also known as the Social Security Benefit Statement, that summarizes the amount of benefits you received for the year. A worksheet (IRS Notice 703) is also enclosed so you can figure out whether any portion of your benefits is subject to income tax.

MEDICARE

If you have been receiving SSDI benefits for two years, you will automatically be enrolled in Medicare. Three months before your eligibility goes into effect, you will receive a Medicare health insurance card that contains your name, Medicare claim number, effective date, and the benefits to which you're entitled. Sign the card and carry it with you at all times.

Medicare consists of two types of insurance: hospital and medical. Hospital insurance helps pay hospital bills and some follow-up care. This coverage is "premium-free" since the taxes you paid while working finance this coverage.

Medical insurance helps pay doctors' bills and other services; however, there is a monthly premium for this coverage, which is deducted from your monthly award. Currently, the monthly premium is $42.50. Federal law requires that state Medicaid programs pay Medicare costs for certain elderly and disabled people with low incomes and very limited resources; check with your local SSA office to see if you qualify.

You will receive a statement showing payments made to doctors and hospitals once you begin to use your Medicare coverage. Begin keeping a file of all of your statements so you can keep track of all the services Medicare pays for. Since you have to pay a portion of the medical insurance, consider obtaining additional insurance such as a "Medigap" policy. Contact your local SSA office for more information.

MEDICAID/MEDI-CAL

If you are approved for SSI benefits, you will be eligible to receive Medicaid or Medi-Cal. Medicaid is a public health program for SSI recipients as well as for people who have no or very little income. Under Medicaid, certain hospital and medical expenses are paid for from state and federal funds. These expenses include inpatient and outpatient hospital expenses, laboratory and x-ray services, and physician services.

Medi-Cal is a state assistance program for individuals in California who receive *any* of the following benefits:

- Aid to Families with Dependent Children (AFDC)
- Supplemental Security Income (SSI)
- Entrant Cash Assistance (ECA); Refugee Cash Assistance (RCA)
- In-Home Supportive Services (IHSS)

An individual may also receive Medi-Cal if he/she has limited resources and is at least *one* of the following:

- Age 65 or older or under the age of 21
- Disabled
- Blind
- Pregnant
- A member of a family who meets federal AFDC deprivation requirements
- Currently receiving care in a skilled-nursing or intermediate-care facility
- A refugee or entrant who has been in the country less than 12 months

Medi-Cal also provides special benefits for individuals who:

- Lose their eligibility for SSI benefits because of cost-of-living increases in their regular Social Security disability or retirement benefits
- Are eligible for Medicare and need help to pay their Medicare premiums, deductibles, and coinsurance
- Need renal dialysis because of loss of kidney function or parenteral hyperalimentation because he/she cannot digest food

Under Medi-Cal, individuals receive coverage for the following services:

- Office visits
- Hospital and nursing-home care
- Laboratory and x-ray services
- Mental-health services
- Prescriptions and medications
- Eyeglasses, hearing aids, medical supplies, and equipment ordered by your doctor
- Special checkups for children under 21 through the Child Health and Disability Prevention Program (CHDP)

Contact SSA for more information including eligibility requirements for both the Medicaid and Medi-Cal programs.

VESTED RIGHT IN A RETIREMENT/DISABILITY PLAN

If you had a vested right in a retirement plan with your employer, check to see if you can apply for retirement benefits if you are permanently disabled and qualify for SSDI benefits. You may also be entitled to hospital and medical insurance, dental and eye care, and prescription coverage.

LOW-INCOME STATUS

Once you are found to be eligible for disability benefits, contact your local utility companies and inquire how you can apply for low-income status. If you qualify, you will receive lower rates. In addition, if your doctor prescribes an electric hospital bed, oxygen concentrator, or other electrical medical equipment, you may be entitled to an increase in your electrical usage. Contact your local electric company for more information.

CORRECTING YOUR EARNINGS RECORDS

Social Security benefits are based upon a worker's earnings as reported to SSA. For this reason, it is important for these earnings to be reported to SSA promptly and accurately. SSA compiles your earnings record from the information reported on W-2 forms supplied by your employers.

You should check on your own Social Security earnings record every three years by completing a Request for Earnings and Benefit Estimate Statement (Form SSA-7004SM). This form is available free of charge at your local SSA office. Upon completion, you will receive a Personal Earnings and Benefit Estimate Statement that will show the following:

1. Total earnings credited to the record beginning January 1, 1937, through December 31, 1950
2. Annual totals of earnings for the years 1951 through the second year immediately preceding the current year
3. Number of quarters of coverage needed for an insured status and the number of quarters of coverage credited to the record
4. Various benefit estimates

If you find that some earnings have not been credited, contact SSA and ask how you can correct your records. The time limit for correcting one's record is set by law at three years, three months, and 15 days after the year in which the wages were paid or the self-employment income was earned. Usually SSA will check if any missing reports of earnings can be located; if they cannot be located, SSA will write your employer and request an earnings statement. Your earnings record will be corrected if your employer(s) submits a signed statement, a W-2 form, pay envelopes, pay slips, or personal records of your wages. If you are self-employed, you may submit a copy of your tax return along with applicable schedules and evidence that the return had been filed timely with the IRS. This evidence may include canceled checks or IRS receipts. If a partnership is involved, a copy of Form 1065 should be furnished.

If you and your employer disagree about the amount of wages paid or when they were paid, SSA will help to obtain evidence to settle the matter. A decision will then be made as to whether the earnings can be credited, the amount of the earnings, and the period to which they should be credited.

PROPERTY TAXES

Some states offer tax-assistance and tax-postponement programs for the disabled and blind. For example, California's Gonsalves-Deukmejian-Petris Citizens Property Tax Assistance Law provides direct cash reimbursement for a portion of the property taxes on homes that have a total household income of $13,200 or less and are occupied by individuals who are 62 or older, blind, or disabled.

In addition, California's Senior Citizens Property Tax Postponement Law gives qualified persons who are 62 or older, blind, or disabled with a household income of $24,000 or less ($34,000 or less for those claimants who filed and qualified for the 1983–84 fiscal year) the option of having the state pay all or part of the taxes on their homes. The amount of taxes postponed must be repaid. Check if your state offers similar tax-assistance and tax-postponement programs.

Chapter 9

RECONSIDERATION APPEAL

If you are dissatisfied with the initial determination that was made on your case, you may file a written request for a reconsideration within 60 days from the date you received your decision letter. Contact your local SSA office in person or by mail and request a reconsideration appeals package, which should consist of the following forms:

- Request for Reconsideration
- Reconsideration Disability Report
- Authorization for Source to Release Information to SSA

A sample of each form may be found at the end of this chapter.

WHAT IF I CAN'T FILE FOR A RECONSIDERATION ON TIME?

If you are unable to meet the filing date, you may ask SSA for an extension. Your request must be in writing and must provide a valid reason(s) why you missed the deadline. Examples of valid reasons are the following:

- You were seriously ill and could not contact SSA in writing or through a friend, relative, or other person.
- There was a death or serious illness in your immediate family.

- Important records were destroyed or damaged by a fire or by other accidental circumstances.
- You were trying but were unable to support your claim within the stated time period.
- You did not receive a determination letter.
- You sent the request to another government agency, in good faith, within the time limit, and the request did not reach SSA until after the time period had expired.
- Unusual or unavoidable circumstances exist that show that you could not have known of the need to file on time or that prevented you from filing.

When you complete and submit your reconsideration application package, SSA sends it back to the Disability Determination Section (DDS), where a new examiner is appointed to look at your case. Additional medical records will be requested if you've visited any new doctors since your initial claim. As previously mentioned, submitting these records with your package will save valuable time. In addition, the DDS examiner may request that you attend additional medical appointments.

It is not necessary for you to hire an attorney or a representative at the reconsideration appeal level. The forms you are to submit are both minimal and straightforward, and the daily diary that you've been keeping will help you complete them. If your condition has worsened since the time you submitted your initial application, stress this in the Reconsideration Disability Report and in the cover letter you will enclose with your reconsideration application package.

Lastly, if you need more room to answer any question, use a separate sheet of paper and head it with your name, Social Security number, and the question you are answering. Also, make sure to sign and date all forms.

REQUEST FOR RECONSIDERATION FORM (EXHIBIT I)

At the top of the form, fill in:

- Your name (or the name of the claimant, if different)
- Name of the wage earner or self-employed person (if different from the claimant)

- Your Social Security number
- Your SSI claim number
- Your spouse's name and Social Security number (only in SSI cases)

On the next few lines indicate whether your claim was for SSDI or SSI benefits and explain why you don't agree with the initial determination made on your case. Your explanation should mention that you are still disabled and unable to work and should include a description of your ongoing physical or mental problems.

Complete the next section only if you are applying for an SSI reconsideration. Read the back of the form and then check one of the three ways you may appeal: case review, informal conference, or formal conference. You should check the case review box so that your claim will be reviewed three to six months sooner than it would be reviewed in a hearing. SSDI cases are always evaluated by a case review.

Fill in the rest of the form with your name, address, and telephone number. If you are the claimant's representative, fill in both your and the claimant's name, address, and telephone number. After completing the form, send the top original to SSA and keep the carbon copy for your files.

RECONSIDERATION DISABILITY REPORT (EXHIBIT J)

At the top of the form, fill in the date you filed your initial claim.

Part I. Information About Your Condition

The questions in this section refer to your condition since you filed your initial claim.

1. Describe any changes in your medical condition.
2. Describe any physical or mental limitations you developed as a result of your condition since you filed your claim.
3. If your physician has placed any restrictions on you, provide the name, address, and telephone number of the physician and note what kinds of restrictions have been placed on you.
4. Describe any additional illness or injury you may have developed, along with the date it occurred.

Part II. Information About Your Medical Records

5. If you have seen any physician since you filed your claim, provide his or her name, address, and telephone number. Also indicate how often you see this physician, the date(s) you saw him or her, the reasons for your visits, and the type of treatment you received. You should also mention if the medications you are taking have changed in any way.
6. If you have seen any other physician, fill in the same information that was requested in item 5. If you have been to more physicians, list their names, addresses, dates, and reasons for visits in Part V.
7. Indicate if you have been hospitalized or treated at a clinic or confined in a nursing home or extended-care facility for your disabling condition. Provide the name, address, and telephone number of the hospital or other facility. Indicate if you were an inpatient and fill in the dates of your admissions and discharges. If you were an outpatient, fill in the dates of your visits. Lastly, provide the reason for your hospitalization, clinic visits, or confinement as well as the type of treatment you received. If you have been to other hospitals, clinics, or extended-care facilities, provide the same information in Part V.
8. Indicate if you have been seen by other agencies for your condition, such as welfare or vocational rehabilitation agencies. If you have, provide the name and address of the agency, your claim number, the dates of visits, and the name of the counselor or social worker you met. Also describe the type of treatment or examination you received. If you need more space, list the other agencies in Part V.

Part III. Information About Work

9. Indicate if you have worked since you filed your claim. Since you are filing for disability benefits and are trying to prove that you are incapable of doing any kind of work, your answer should be no. However, if you did work, you must state so, since SSA will find out if appropriate taxes were taken out of your wages.

Part IV. Information About Your Activities

10. Indicate how your illness or injury affects your ability to care for your personal needs.

11. Indicate what changes have occurred in your daily activities since you filed your claim.

Part V. Remarks and Authorizations

This section authorizes SSA to release copies of your medical records to any new medical source and to the state vocational rehabilitation agency. If you consent to having your records released and find no exceptions to the provisions listed, write "none" in the space provided. In item 12b, write the telephone number where you can be reached and the best time to contact you.

Use page 4 of the application to add additional information for any of the previous questions or to add any new information. Remember that you want to use the reconsideration appeal level to supply new information about your condition or supply data that were originally left out of your paperwork.

Once you have completed this form, be sure to sign and date it and make a copy for your files. Witnesses are required only if the form is marked "X". If the form is marked "X", two witnesses who know the claimant must sign and date the form as well as provide their full addresses.

AUTHORIZATION FOR SOURCE TO RELEASE INFORMATION TO SSA (EXHIBIT K)

By signing this form, you authorize your medical source to release your medical records or other information regarding your treatment and/or hospitalization to SSA. You also agree to permit your medical source to release information about how your impairment affects your ability to work and complete daily tasks and activities. Sign the bottom of the form and fill in your name, address, and telephone number.

COVER LETTER

Once you have completed the entire reconsideration application package, write a cover letter to be enclosed with it. Following is a sample:

Susan Jones
200 Main St.
Baltimore, MD 21200

April 1, 1995

RE: Request for Reconsideration Appeal
SS# 545-26-2431

Social Security Administration
2000 Oak St.
Los Angeles, CA 90210

Dear Gentlemen:

My original claim for disability benefits was denied, therefore I am writing to appeal my case. Enclosed you will find the following completed, signed and dated forms:

Request For Reconsideration

Reconsideration Disability Report

Authorization For Source To Release Information To SSA

New doctor reports (if any)

In the denial letter I received, you stated_____.[Explain here why SSA denied your claim.]

I, however, still suffer from_____[List here your disabilities.] and am unable to do my past work or any other type of work. [This paragraph is important since you want to mention any impairment you left out of your original paperwork and any new illnesses or injuries that you've developed. Also make sure to elaborate on why you are unable to work, for instance you may still suffer from pain.]

I would appreciate you reconsidering my case as soon as possible. Thank you for your cooperation in this matter.

Sincerely,

Susan Jones

You will receive a written notice once a decision has been made on your reconsideration appeal. The determination made is binding unless you file for an administrative law judge appeal.

Reconsideration Appeal 143

EXHIBIT I

Request for Reconsideration

DEPARTMENT OF HEALTH AND HUMAN SERVICES
SOCIAL SECURITY ADMINISTRATION

REQUEST FOR RECONSIDERATION

TOE 710

(Do not write in this space)

The information on this form is authorized by regulation (20 CFR 404.907 – 404.921 and 416.1407 – 416.1421). While your responses to these questions is voluntary, the Social Security Administration cannot reconsider the decision on this claim unless the information is furnished.

NAME OF CLAIMANT

NAME OF WAGE EARNER OR SELF-EMPLOYED PERSON *(If different from claimant.)*

SOCIAL SECURITY CLAIM NUMBER

SUPPLEMENTAL SECURITY INCOME (SSI) CLAIM NUMBER

SPOUSE'S NAME *(Complete ONLY in SSI cases)*

SPOUSE'S SOCIAL SECURITY NUMBER *(Complete ONLY in SSI cases)*

CLAIM FOR *(Specify type, e.g., retirement, disability, hospital insurance, SSI, etc.)*

I do not agree with the determination made on the above claim and request reconsideration. My reasons are:

SUPPLEMENTAL SECURITY INCOME RECONSIDERATION ONLY *(See reverse of claimant's copy)*

"I want to appeal your decision about my claim for supplemental security income, SSI. I've read the back of this form about the three ways to appeal. I've checked the box below."

☐ Case Review ☐ Informal Conference ☐ Formal Conference

EITHER THE CLAIMANT OR REPRESENTATIVE SHOULD SIGN – ENTER ADDRESSES FOR BOTH

SIGNATURE OR NAME OF CLAIMANT'S REPRESENTATIVE
☐ NON-ATTORNEY
☐ ATTORNEY

CLAIMANT SIGNATURE

STREET ADDRESS

STREET ADDRESS

CITY   STATE   ZIP CODE

CITY   STATE   ZIP CODE

TELEPHONE NUMBER *(Include area code)*
(___ ___ ___)   DATE

TELEPHONE NUMBER *(Include area code)*
(___ ___ ___)   DATE

TO BE COMPLETED BY SOCIAL SECURITY ADMINISTRATION

See reverse of claim folder copy for list of initial determinations

1. HAS INITIAL DETERMINATION BEEN MADE?   ☐ YES   ☐ NO

2. CLAIMANT INSISTS ON FILING   ☐ YES   ☐ NO

3. IS THIS REQUEST FILED TIMELY?   ☐ YES   ☐ NO
(If "NO", attach claimant's explanation for delay and attach only pertinent letter, material, or information in social security office.)

RETIREMENT AND SURVIVORS RECONSIDERATIONS ONLY (CHECK ONE) REFER TO (GN 03102.125)

SOCIAL SECURITY OFFICE ADDRESS

☐ NO FURTHER DEVELOPMENT REQUIRED   (GN 03102.125)

☐ REQUIRED DEVELOPMENT ATTACHED

☐ REQUIRED DEVELOPMENT PENDING, WILL FORWARD OR ADVISE STATUS WITHIN 30 DAYS

ROUTING INSTRUCTIONS (CHECK ONE)
☐ DISABILITY DETERMINATION SERVICES *(ROUTE WITH DISABILITY FOLDER)*
☐ INTPSC, BALTIMORE
☐ ODO, BALTIMORE
☐ DISTRICT OFFICE RECONSIDERATION
☐ PROGRAM SERVICE CENTER
☐ OCRO BALTIMORE

NOTE: TAKE OR MAIL COMPLETED COPIES TO YOUR SOCIAL SECURITY OFFICE

FORM **SSA-561-U2** (9-85)

CLAIMS FOLDER

144 *How You Can Apply for Social Security Disability Benefits*

EXHIBIT J

Reconsideration Disability Report

DEPARTMENT OF HEALTH AND HUMAN SERVICES
Social Security Administration

Form Approved
OMB No. 0960-0144

For SSA Use Only - Do NOT Complete This Item.	
Name of Wage Earner	Social Security Number
Name of Claimant	Social Security Number
Type of Claim:	
Title II — ☐ Freeze ☐ DIB ☐ DWB ☐ CDB	Title XVI — ☐ Disability ☐ Blind ☐ Child

RECONSIDERATION DISABILITY REPORT

PLEASE PRINT, TYPE OR WRITE CLEARLY AND ANSWER ALL ITEMS TO THE BEST OF YOUR ABILITY. If you are filing on behalf of someone else, answer all questions. COMPLETE ANSWERS WILL AID IN PROCESSING THE CLAIM.

PRIVACY ACT/PAPERWORK REDUCTION ACT NOTICE: The Social Security Administration is authorized to collect the information on this form under sections 205(a), 223(d) and 1633(a) of the Social Security Act. The information on this form is needed by Social Security to make a decision on your claim. While giving us the information on this form is voluntary, failure to provide all or part of the requested information could prevent an accurate or timely decision on your claim and could result in the loss of benefits. Although the information you furnish on this form is almost never used for any purpose other than making a determination on your disability claim, such information may be disclosed by the Social Security Administration as follows: (1) To enable a third party or agency to assist Social Security in establishing rights to Social Security benefits and/or coverage; (2) to comply with Federal laws requiring the release of information from Social Security records (e.g., the General Accounting Office and the Veterans Administration); (3) to facilitate statistical research and audit activities necessary to assure the integrity and improvement of the Social Security programs (e.g., to the Bureau of the Census and private concerns under contract to Social Security). These and other reasons why information about you may be used or given out are explained in the **Federal Register**. If you would like more information about this, any Social Security office can assist you.

Date Claim Filed

PART I — INFORMATION ABOUT YOUR CONDITION

1. Has there been any change (for better or worse) in your illness or injury since you filed your claim? .... ☐ Yes ☐ No
   If "Yes," describe any changes in your symptoms.

2. Describe any physical or mental limitations you have as a result of your condition since you filed your claim.

3. Have any restrictions been placed on you by a physician since you filed your claim? .... ☐ Yes ☐ No
   If "Yes," give name, address, and telephone number of the physician and show what kinds of restrictions have been imposed.

4. Do you have any additional illness or injury that you feel we should know about? .... ☐ Yes ☐ No
   If "Yes," describe the kind of illness or injury and the date that it occurred.

FORM SSA-3441-F6 (2-88)

Reconsideration Appeal 145

PART II — INFORMATION ABOUT YOUR MEDICAL RECORDS

5. Have you seen any physician since you filed your claim? .... ☐ Yes ☐ No
If "Yes," provide the following about the physician you last visited:

NAME	ADDRESS (Include ZIP Code)
AREA CODE AND TELEPHONE NUMBER	
HOW OFTEN DO YOU SEE THIS PHYSICIAN?	DATE YOU SAW THIS PHYSICIAN

REASONS FOR VISITS

TYPE OF TREATMENT RECEIVED *(Include drugs, surgery, tests)*

6. Have you see any other physician since you filed your claim? .... ☐ Yes ☐ No
If "Yes," show the following:

NAME	ADDRESS (Include ZIP Code)
AREA CODE AND TELEPHONE NUMBER	
HOW OFTEN DO YOU SEE THIS PHYSICIAN?	DATE YOU SAW THIS PHYSICIAN

REASONS FOR VISITS

TYPE OF TREATMENT RECEIVED *(Include drugs, surgery, tests)*

If you have seen other physicians since you filed your claim, list their names, addresses, dates and reasons for visits in Part V.

7. Have you been hospitalized, or treated at a clinic or confined in a nursing home or extended care facility for your illness or injury since you filed your claim? .... ☐ Yes ☐ No
If "Yes," show the following:

NAME OF FACILITY	ADDRESS OF AGENCY (Include ZIP Code)
PATIENT OR CLINIC NUMBER	
WERE YOU AN INPATIENT? *(Stayed at least overnight)* ☐ Yes ☐ No IF "YES," SHOW ⟶	DATES OF ADMISSIONS AND DISCHARGES
WERE YOU AN OUTPATIENT? ☐ Yes ☐ No IF "YES," SHOW ⟶	DATES OF VISITS

REASON FOR HOSPITALIZATION, CLINIC VISITS, OR CONFINEMENT

TYPE OF TREATMENT RECEIVED *(Include drugs, surgery, tests)*

If you have been in other hospitals, clinics, nursing homes, or extended care facilities for your illness or injury, list the names, addresses, patient or clinic numbers, dates and reasons for hospitalization, clinic visits, or confinement in Part V.

8. Have you been seen by other agencies for your injury or illness? .... ☐ Yes ☐ No
(VA, Workmen's Compensation, Vocational Rehabilitation, Welfare, Special Schools, Unions, etc.)
If "Yes," show the following:

NAME OF AGENCY	ADDRESS OF AGENCY (Include ZIP Code)
YOUR CLAIM NUMBER	
DATES OF VISITS	NAME OF COUNSELOR, SOCIAL WORKER, ETC.

TYPE OF TREATMENT OR EXAMINATION RECEIVED *(Include drugs, surgery, tests)*

If more space is needed, list the other agencies, their addresses, your claim numbers, dates, and treatment received in Part V.

FORM **SSA-3441-F6** (2-88)

146 *How You Can Apply for Social Security Disability Benefits*

PART III — INFORMATION ABOUT WORK

9. Have you worked since you filed your claim? .... ☐ Yes ☐ No

   If "Yes," you will be asked to give details on a separate form.

PART IV — INFORMATION ABOUT YOUR ACTIVITIES

10. How does your illness or injury affect your ability to care for your personal needs?

11. What changes have occurred in your daily activities since you filed your claim?
    (If none, show, "None")

PART V — REMARKS AND AUTHORIZATIONS

12.(a) READ CAREFULLY: I authorize the Social Security Administration to release information from my records, as necessary to process my claim, as follows:

   Copies of my medical records may be furnished to a physician or a medical institution for background information if it is necessary for me to have a medical examination by that physician or medical institution. The results of any such examination may be given to my personal physician.

   Information from my records may also be furnished, if necessary, to any company providing clerical and administrative services for the purposes of transcribing, typing, copying or otherwise clerically servicing such information. The State Vocational Rehabilitation Agency may also have access to information in my records to determine my eligibility for rehabilitative services.

   I understand and concur with the statement and authorizations given above, except as follows (If there are no exceptions, write "None" in the space below. If you do not concur with any part of the above statement, state your objections clearly):

12.(b)	Telephone number where you can be reached:	Best time to reach you:

FORM **SSA-3441-F6** (2-88)　　　3

Reconsideration Appeal 147

12.(b) Use this section to continue information required by prior sections. Identify the section for which the information is provided. Note: This section may also be used for any special or additional information which you wish to be recorded.

_____

_____

_____

_____

_____

_____

_____

_____

_____

_____

_____

_____

_____

_____

_____

_____

_____

_____

_____

_____

_____

_____

_____

We may also use the information you give us when we match records by computer. Matching programs compare our records with those of other Federal, State, or local government agencies. Many agencies may use matching programs to find or prove that a person qualifies for benefits paid by the Federal government. The law allows us to do this even if you do not agree to it.

These and other reasons why information about you may be used or given out are explained in the *Federal Register*. If you want to learn more about this, contact any Social Security office.

TIME IT TAKES TO COMPLETE THIS FORM

We estimate that it will take you about 30 minutes to complete this form. This includes the time it will take to read the instructions, gather the necessary facts and fill out the form. If you have comments or suggestions on this estimate, or on any other aspect of this form, write to the Social Security Administration, ATTN: Reports Clearance Officer, 1-A-21 Operations Bldg., Baltimore, MD 21235-0001, and to the Office of Management and Budget, Paperwork Reduction Project (0960-0144), Washington, D.C. 20503. **Send only comments relating to our estimate or other aspects of this form to the offices listed above. All requests for Social Security cards and other claims-related information should be sent to your local Social Security office, whose address is listed in your telephone directory under the Department of Health and Human Services.**

Knowing that anyone making a false statement or representation of a material fact for use in determining a right to payment under the Social Security Act commits a crime punishable under Federal Law, I certify that the above statements are true.

NAME (SIGNATURE OF CLAIMANT OR PERSON FILING ON THE CLAIMANT'S BEHALF)	DATE
SIGN HERE ▶	

Witnesses are required ONLY if this statement has been signed by mark (X) above. If signed by mark (X), two witnesses to the signing who know the person making the statement must sign below, giving their full addresses.

1. Signature of Witness	2. Signature of Witness
Address *(Number and street, city, state, and ZIP code)*	Address *(Number and street, city, state, and ZIP code)*

FORM **SSA-3441-F6** (2-88)

148 *How You Can Apply for Social Security Disability Benefits*

EXHIBIT K

Authorization for Source to Release Information to the Social Security Administration (SSA)

RESIDENTS OF CALIFORNIA

I further authorize, by my signature below, a private photocopy company as approved by the Social Security Administration or the State Agency, to photocopy all medical records needed as evidence in determining my eligibility for SSA and/or SSI benefits. I also understand that I have a right to receive a copy of this authorization upon request. Copy requested and received.

☐ Yes ☐ No

TO BE COMPLETED BY SSA
NUMBER HOLDER

SOCIAL SECURITY NUMBER

EMPLOYEE/CLAIMANT/BENEFICIARY *(If other than Number Holder)*

AUTHORIZATION FOR SOURCE TO RELEASE INFORMATION TO THE SOCIAL SECURITY ADMINISTRATION (SSA)

INFORMATION ABOUT SOURCE — PLEASE PRINT, TYPE, OR WRITE CLEARLY

NAME AND ADDRESS OF SOURCE *(Include Zip Code)*	RELATIONSHIP TO CLAIMANT/BENEFICIARY

INFORMATION ABOUT CLAIMANT/BENEFICIARY — PLEASE PRINT, TYPE, OR WRITE CLEARLY

NAME AND ADDRESS *(If known)* AT TIME CLAIMANT/BENEFICIARY HAD CONTACT WITH SOURCE *(Include Zip Code)*	DATE OF BIRTH	CLAIMANT/BENEFICIARY I.D. NUMBER *(If known and different than SSN) (Clinic/Patient No.)*

APPROXIMATE DATES OF CLAIMANT/BENEFICIARY CONTACT WITH SOURCE *(e.g., dates of hospital admission, treatment, discharge, etc.)*

TO BE COMPLETED BY CLAIMANT/BENEFICIARY OR PERSON AUTHORIZED TO ACT IN HIS/HER BEHALF

GENERAL AND SPECIAL AUTHORIZATION TO RELEASE MEDICAL AND OTHER INFORMATION IN ACCORDANCE WITH THE PROVISIONS OF THE SOCIAL SECURITY ACT; THE PUBLIC HEALTH SERVICE ACT, SECTIONS 523 AND 527; AND TITLE 38 U.S.C. VETERANS BENEFITS, SECTION 4132.

I hereby authorize the above-named source to release or disclose to the Social Security Administration or State agency the following information for the period(s) identified above:

1) All medical records or other information regarding my treatment, hospitalization, and/or outpatient care for my impairment(s), including psychological or psychiatric impairment(s), drug abuse, alcoholism, sickle cell anemia, acquired immunodeficiency syndrome (AIDS), or tests for or infection with human immunodeficiency virus (HIV);

2) Information about how my impairment(s) affects my ability to complete tasks and activities of daily living;

3) Information about how my impairment(s) affected my ability to work.

I understand that this authorization, except for action already taken, may be voided by me at anytime. If I do not void this authorization, it will automatically end when a final decision is made on my claim. If I am already receiving benefits, the authorization will end when a final decision is made as to whether I can continue to receive benefits.

READ IMPORTANT INFORMATION ON REVERSE BEFORE SIGNING FORM BELOW.

SIGNATURE OF CLAIMANT/BENEFICIARY OR PERSON AUTHORIZED TO ACT IN HIS/HER BEHALF	RELATIONSHIP TO CLAIMANT/BENEFICIARY *(If other than self)*	DATE

STREET ADDRESS	TELEPHONE NUMBER *(Area Code)*	

CITY	STATE	ZIP CODE

The signature and address of a person who either knows the person signing this form or is satistifed as to that person's identity is requested below. This is not required by the Social Security Administration, but without it the source may not honor this authorization.

SIGNATURE OF WITNESS	STREET ADDRESS	

CITY	STATE	ZIP CODE

Form SSA-827-OP1 (7-92) Use Prior Editions **(OVER)**

Chapter 10

ADMINISTRATIVE LAW JUDGE APPEAL

If your reconsideration was denied, you may further appeal your case by filing an administrative law judge (ALJ) appeal within 60 days from the date you received the decision letter. If you are unable to meet the filing date, you may ask SSA for an extension. Your request must be in writing and must provide a valid reason(s) why you missed the deadline. (The examples of valid reasons used for reconsideration appeals in chapter 9 may be used here as well.) Contact your local SSA office and request an ALJ appeals package, which should consist of the following forms:

- Request for Hearing by Administrative Law Judge
- Claimant's Statement When Request for Hearing Is Filed and the Issue Is Disability
- Authorization for Source to Release Information to SSA

A sample of each form may be found at the end of this chapter.

You may submit new evidence at the ALJ appeal level and examine the evidence that was used to make the determination on your case. You also have the option of attending an oral hearing before the administrative law judge or having a decision made based on the evidence in your case. At the ALJ hearing, you may explain in person the details of your case and have the opportunity to present witnesses. ALJ hearings will be further discussed later in this chapter.

At the ALJ appeal level, 60 to 70 percent of denied cases are approved. One reason for this high approval rate is that you, or a representative whom you appoint, can review your claim file produced by SSA. By examining your file, you will be able to ensure that none of the pertinent information about your impairment and your inability to work was overlooked, undervalued, misinterpreted, or relayed inaccurately. You will also have the opportunity to identify which evidence is still needed to gain a favorable determination.

REPRESENTATION

SSA recognizes a person as your representative if both you and your chosen representative sign an Appointment of Representative form, which will be sent to you by SSA upon request. Your representative will receive copies of any administrative actions, including determinations and decisions made on your case. He/she will also receive requests for information or evidence. In essence, a notice sent to your representative will have the same force and effect as if it had been sent to you.

A representative, on your behalf, is permitted to do all of the following:

- Obtain information about your claim to the same extent you are able to
- Submit evidence
- Make statements about facts and law
- Make any request or give any notice about the proceedings before SSA

A representative, however, may *not* sign an application on your behalf for rights or benefits, unless authorized to do so.

When choosing a representative, keep in mind that he/she may be an attorney, a family member, or a friend. If you decide to hire an attorney, he/she must:

- Have the right to practice law before a court of a state, territory, district, or island possession of the United States or before the Supreme Court or a lower federal court of the United States

- Not be disqualified or suspended from acting as a representative in dealings with SSA
- Not be prohibited by any law from acting as a representative

If you decide to appoint a representative who is not an attorney, he/she must:

- Be generally known to have a good character and reputation
- Be capable of giving valuable help to you in connection with your claim
- Not be disqualified or suspended from acting as a representative in dealing with SSA
- Not be prohibited by any law from acting as a representative

Representatives may charge a fee for their services if they file an Approval of Fee form with SSA after the proceedings in which he/she represented you are completed. The fee payable in any claim is determined by SSA. SSA may authorize a fee even if you do not receive benefits. After the fee to be charged is determined, SSA will notify both you and your representative of the approved charge and how it made its decision. SSA is not responsible for paying the fee.

One main difference between hiring an attorney and hiring a relative or friend is that an attorney may charge up to 25 percent of your retroactive benefits. For example, if your monthly award is $600, your retroactive benefits for 12 months would total $7,200. Your attorney could receive 25 percent of this, or $1,800. Also, keep in mind that a majority of attorneys do not take disability cases unless the case has reached the ALJ appeal level. Therefore, not only do you give up a significant portion of your disability benefits to an attorney, but you are also paying him/her an exorbitant amount for assistance only in the very last stages of the disability claims process. Read this entire chapter before deciding to spend so much money on an attorney; you won't have to hire one if you know how to prepare yourself.

THE HEARING

As mentioned earlier, you may decide to appeal your case by requesting a hearing before an administrative law judge. At the hearing, you may present witnesses and explain in detail how your impairment(s) prevents you from working and performing daily activities. You will be notified of the time and place of the hearing at least 20 days before the scheduled date.

WHAT IF I CAN'T ATTEND A SCHEDULED HEARING?

If you cannot attend a hearing, you must notify the administrative law judge immediately. Your objection must be based on one of the reasons listed below and must be accompanied with an alternative time and place.

- You or your representative are unable to attend or travel to the hearing because of a serious physical or mental condition or a death in the family.
- Severe weather conditions make it impossible for you to travel to the hearing.
- You have attempted to obtain a representative, but need additional time.
- Your representative was appointed within 30 days of the hearing and needs additional time to prepare for the hearing.
- Your representative has to be in court or attend another ALJ hearing on the scheduled date.
- A material witness is unable to attend the hearing.
- Transportation is not readily available for you to travel to the hearing.
- You are illiterate and as a result were unable to respond to the notice of a hearing.

An administrative law judge cannot conduct a hearing if he/she is partial to any party or has any personal interest in the matter pending for decision. If you object to the judge who will conduct your hearing, notify him/her as soon as possible. The judge will consider your objections and decide whether to withdraw from the hearing. If he/she withdraws, the associate commissioner for hearings and appeals will appoint another administrative law judge to conduct the hearing. If the judge you object to does not withdraw, you may, after the hearing, present your objections to the Appeals Council as reasons why a new hearing before another administrative law judge should be held.

YOUR SSA FILE

As soon as you receive notice about your hearing, contact your local SSA office and request it to send you a copy of your SSA file (you may also examine the file in person). When requesting a copy, insist that you receive it immediately; sometimes SSA asks claimants to wait until the day of the hearing to review their files. You want to give yourself ample time before the hearing to review your files and to determine what evidence is still needed.

Your SSA file includes copies of the following documents:

- Disability application
- Notice of initial denial
- Reconsideration application
- Notice of reconsideration denial
- ALJ application
- Waiver of oral hearing
- Representative form
- Earnings record
- Work activity report
- Workers' compensation information
- Medical history
- Daily activities report (claimant)
- Daily activities report (third party)
- Report of contact
  This form is used by SSA to record telephone conversations between you and an SSA examiner. Examine this form carefully and make sure that everything is relayed accurately. If necessary, refer to your daily diary, which should include a record of all contact between you and SSA. If something in the report is erroneous and/or misleading, make a note for yourself to address this in the argument letter you will submit to the judge.
- Chest pain questionnaire
- Disability determination by state agency (DDS)
  Pay close attention to the Medical/Vocational Decision Guide sheet included with this form. SSA uses this form to indicate what kind of work you are capable of doing despite your impairment: sedentary, light, medium, heavy, or very heavy work. The form also includes your past job titles, SSA job code

descriptions, your age, amount of education or vocational training you have, and your ability to communicate in English. Make sure that everything stated about your vocational history is correct.
- Consultative reports from SSA-appointed doctors
These reports summarize what occurred at your doctor appointment(s). If you feel you did not have an adequate examination by a physician, mention this in your letter to the judge. The judge may decide to reschedule an appointment for you with another doctor if he/she deems it would be helpful to your claim.
- Claimant's work background
- Claimant's medications

What will I be asked at the hearing?

Since each hearing is conducted differently, there are no set questions. However, below are some sample questions that you may be asked:

- What is your impairment(s)?
- When did your disability begin? How has it worsened?
- How does your disability affect your ability to work and perform normal daily activities? (Present medical evidence that supports each restriction you have. Include doctors' statements or notes, hospital admission records, operative notes, and written statements from individuals who have witnessed your restrictions and can confirm your condition.)

Consider presenting a written statement that summarizes everything you want to relay to the judge at the hearing. Do not allow the judge or any of the proceedings to intimidate you, especially if you are representing yourself. Simply answer the questions as thoroughly and explicitly as you can.

You might have to attend another scheduled doctor's appointment if the judge decides that more medical evidence is needed. Your claim will be denied if you fail to attend a scheduled appointment. The judge has 90 days from when he/she receives the physician's medical evaluation to issue a decision.

What if I don't want to attend a hearing?

It is not necessary for you to request a hearing. Instead, you may ask that the administrative law judge base his/her decision on the evidence in your case. Since hearings take anywhere from three to four months to be scheduled, the biggest advantage of not requesting a hearing is that a determination on your case will be made sooner. In addition, not having to address a judge in person will save you a lot of stress and anxiety!

In order to have your case reviewed on the basis of its evidence, complete a Waiver of Right to Oral Hearing form, which will be sent to you by SSA upon request. This form will be further discussed later in this chapter. The administrative law judge will review your entire file, including all completed applications, written statements, certificates, reports, affidavits, and other documents that were used in making the determination on your case. The judge will also review any additional evidence you or any other party submit in writing. Basically, your file should include everything that would be presented at a face-to-face hearing, including supporting statements from friends, relatives, and doctors.

In addition, mention in your paperwork if your doctor informed you that after a certain amount of time you would be capable of performing some type of work. A judge would certainly look favorably on your case if you mention that you want to return to the workforce.

Should I include my financial problems in my paperwork to the judge?

A great deal of time has passed by the time you reach the ALJ appeal level. If you are financially strapped, mention this in your paperwork to the judge. Discuss if you may be losing your home to foreclosure, if utility companies are threatening to cut off your service, or if you don't have enough money to get the medical attention you need. But make sure to center your paperwork on the medical facts of your case; never use your financial problems as reasons to apply for disability benefits.

THE APPLICATION

Although you may request to receive the various appeals forms by telephone, put your request in writing to alert SSA immediately that you intend to appeal your case further. Before writing your letter, decide if you want to request a hearing before an administrative law judge. As previously mentioned, you can expedite the ALJ appeals process by having your case reviewed on the basis of its records. Following is a sample letter:

Susan Jones
200 Main St.
Baltimore, MD 21200

May 1, 1995

RE: REQUEST FOR ALJ APPEAL
SS#: 545-26-2431

Social Security Administration
2000 Oak St.
Los Angeles, CA 90210

Dear Gentlemen:

    I am writing to acknowledge that I have received the Notice of Disapproved Claim, dated_____which informed me that my claim for a reconsideration was denied. Since I am intending to file an administrative law judge appeal, please send me, at your earliest convenience, the following forms: Request for Hearing by Administrative Law Judge, Claimant's Statement When Request for Hearing Is Filed, and the Authorization for Source to Release Information to SSA.

    Since I have decided to waive my right to an oral hearing and instead have my case reviewed "on the record," please send me the Waiver of Right to Oral Hearing form to complete. Once received, I will promptly complete these forms and return them to you to be included in my file.

    Since I have chosen to have my case reviewed on its evidence, please send me a copy of my SSA file. If this is not possible, please notify me as to when I can visit your office to view my file.

    Your prompt attention to this request is greatly appreciated.

Sincerely,

Susan Jones

REQUEST FOR HEARING BY ADMINISTRATIVE LAW JUDGE (EXHIBIT L)

At the top of the form, fill in:

1. Your name (or the name of the claimant, if different)
2. The name of the wage earner (if different)
3. Your Social Security number
4. Your spouse's claim number
5. State why you are requesting a hearing. For instance, you may write that you are still disabled and unable to work.
6. If you have additional evidence to submit, such as medical records, check the appropriate box and send the evidence within 10 days.
7. Indicate if you wish or don't wish to appear at a hearing.
8. Sign your name and fill in your address and telephone number.
9. If you have a representative, have him/her supply the same information as in item 8. Fill in the information if your representative is not available.

CLAIMANT'S STATEMENT WHEN REQUEST FOR HEARING IS FILED AND THE ISSUE IS DISABILITY (EXHIBIT M)

At the top of the form fill in:

- Your name (or the name of the claimant if different) and Social Security number
- The name of the wage earner, if different, and his/her Social Security number

1. Indicate if you worked since you filed your request for a reconsideration. If you did, explain the nature and extent of the work you did.
2. Describe any changes in your condition since the date you filed your reconsideration.
3. Describe any changes in your daily activities and/or social functioning since you filed your reconsideration.
4. If you have been treated or examined by a physician since you filed your reconsideration, provide the physician's name and

address, the date you saw him/her, and the reason for your visit.
5. Indicate if you have been hospitalized since you filed your reconsideration. If you were, provide the hospital's name and address, the date of your hospitalization, and the reason for your hospitalization.
6. Indicate if you received medical or vocational services from a community agency since you filed for reconsideration.
7. If you are taking any prescription drugs or medication, list the name of the medication, the dosage being taken, and the name of the prescribing physician.
8. If you are taking any nonprescription drugs or medication, list the name of the medication and the dosage being taken.

Sign and date the form once you have completed it.

AUTHORIZATION FOR SOURCE TO RELEASE INFORMATION TO SSA (EXHIBIT N)

By signing this form you authorize your medical source to release your medical records or any other information regarding your treatment and/or hospitalization to SSA. You also agree to permit your medical source to release information about how your impairment affects your ability to work and to complete daily tasks and activities. Sign the bottom of the form and fill in your name, address, and telephone number.

WAIVER OF RIGHT TO ORAL HEARING (EXHIBIT O)

You must complete this form if you wish to waive your right to an oral hearing. Below is a sample explanation of why you don't wish to have a hearing:

> *I do not wish to attend a hearing since I want to expedite my case. I herewith request the Social Security office to provide me with a copy of my SSA file or notify me of when I can come to its office to review my SSA file. After my review, I will prepare a written statement and request the administrative law judge to make a decision based on the evidence in my case and on any additional information I provide.*

Once completed, sign and date the form.

APPOINTMENT OF REPRESENTATIVE (EXHIBIT P)

Complete this form if you decide to hire a representative.
At the top of the form, fill in:

- Your name (or the name of the claimant if different) and your Social Security number
- The name of the wage earner (if different) and his/her Social Security number

In Section I provide the name and address of your representative and indicate if you are applying for SSI or SSDI benefits. Sign and date the form and provide your address and telephone number.

In Section II have your representative sign and date the form and fill in his/her address and telephone number.

If your representative decides to waive his/her right to charge you a fee for services rendered, have him/her sign and date Section III.

If your representative only waives his/her right to a direct certification of fee from withheld past-due benefits, but does not waive his/her right to petition for and be authorized to charge and collect a fee, have him/her sign Section III.

THE ADMINISTRATIVE LAW JUDGE'S DECISION

The administrative law judge will issue a written decision on your case based on the evidence offered at the hearing or included in your claim. The judge may also ask the Appeals Council to make a recommended decision. The judge will mail a copy of both his decision and the Appeals Council's recommended decision (if there is one) to you and/or your representative. The judge may also send a copy of his/her decision to the Appeals Council.

If your case is denied at the ALJ appeal level, you may file a Request for Review by the Appeals Council form within 60 days from the date you received the denial letter. The Appeals Council will then decide if your request for a review will be granted, denied, or dismissed. The Appeals Council may also, on its own initiative, decide to review your case.

If the Appeals Council decides to review your case, you or your representative may request an appearance before it to present your oral arguments. The request for an appearance will be granted if the Appeals Council determines that a presentation is needed to render a proper decision. The claimant may also file written statements to support his/her claim.

If your case is denied by the Appeals Council, you may file suit in a federal district court. Your suit must be filed within 60 days from the date you or your representative received notice from the Appeals Council. The federal district court may issue a decision based on the evidence of your case or may request further information. You cannot pursue further court action if the Appeals Council dismissed your request for a review.

Administrative Law Judge Appeal 161

EXHIBIT L
Request for Hearing by Administrative Law Judge

DEPARTMENT OF HEALTH AND HUMAN SERVICES
SOCIAL SECURITY ADMINISTRATION
OFFICE OF HEARINGS AND APPEALS

Form Approved
OMB No. 0960-0269

REQUEST FOR HEARING BY ADMINISTRATIVE LAW JUDGE [Take or mail original and all copies to your local Social Security Office]	**PRIVACY ACT NOTICE** **ON REVERSE SIDE OF FORM.**

1. CLAIMANT	2. WAGE EARNER, IF DIFFERENT	3. SOC. SEC. CLAIM NUMBER	SPOUSE's CLAIM NUMBER

5. I REQUEST A HEARING BEFORE AN ADMINISTRATIVE LAW JUDGE. I disagree with the determination made on my claim because:

You have a right to be represented at the hearing. **If you are not represented but would like to be,** your Social Security Office will give you a list of legal referral and service organizations. (If you are represented, complete form SSA-1696.)

An Administrative Law Judge of the Office of Hearings and Appeals will be appointed to conduct the hearing or other proceedings in your case. You will receive notice of the time and place of a hearing at least 20 days before the day set for a hearing.

6. Check one of these blocks.	7. Check one of the blocks:
☐ I have no additional evidence to submit.	☐ I wish to appear at a hearing.
☐ I have additional evidence to submit. (Please submit it to the Social Security Office within 10 days.)	☐ I do not wish to appear and I request that a decision be made based on the evidence in my case (Complete Waiver Form HA-4608)

[You should complete No. 8 and your representative (if any) should complete No. 9. If you are represented and your representative is not available to complete this form, you should also print his or her name, address, etc. in No. 9.]

8.	9.
(CLAIMANT'S SIGNATURE)	(REPRESENTATIVE'S SIGNATURE/NAME)
ADDRESS	(ADDRESS) ☐ ATTORNEY; ☐ NON ATTORNEY
CITY STATE ZIP CODE	CITY STATE ZIP CODE
DATE AREA CODE AND TELEPHONE NUMBER	DATE AREA CODE AND TELEPHONE NUMBER

TO BE COMPLETED BY SOCIAL SECURITY ADMINISTRATION—ACKNOWLEDGMENT OF REQUEST FOR HEARING

10.
Request for Hearing RECEIVED for the Social Security Administration on _____ by: _____

(TITLE) ADDRESS Servicing FO Code   PC Code

11.
☐ Request timely filed | Request not timely filed-Attach (1) claimant's explanation for delay, (2) any pertinent letter, material, or information in the Social/Security Office.

12. Claimant not represented –
☐ list of legal referral and service organizations provided

13. Interpreter needed –
☐ enter language (including sign language): _____

14.
Check one: ☐ Initial Entitlement Case
☐ Disability Cessation Case
☐ Other Postentitlement Case

15.
Check claim type(s):
☐ RSI only .... (RSI)
☐ Disability—worker or child only .... (DIWC)
☐ Disability—Widow(er) only .... (DIWW)
☐ SSI Aged only .... (SSIA)
☐ SSI Blind only .... (SSIB)
☐ Disability only .... (SSID)
☐ SSI Aged/Title II .... (SSAC)
☐ SSI Blind/Title II .... (SSBC)
☐ SSI Disability/Title II .... (SSDC)
☐ HI Entitlement .... (HIE)
☐ Other—Specify: (_____)

16.
HO COPY SENT TO: _____ HO on _____
☐ CF Attached: ☐ Title II; ☐ Title XVI; or
☐ Title II CF held in FO to establish CAPS ORBIT; or
☐ CF requested: ☐ Title II; ☐ Title XVI
(Copy of teletype or phone report attached).

17.
CF COPY SENT TO: _____ HO on _____
☐ CF attached: ☐ Title II; ☐ Title XVI
☐ Other attached

FORM **HA-501-U5** (5-88)
issue old stock

CLAIMS FOLDER

162 *How You Can Apply for Social Security Disability Benefits*

EXHIBIT M

Claimant's Statement When Request for Hearing Is Filed and the Issue Is Disability

Form Approved
OMB No. 0960-0316

CLAIMANT'S STATEMENT WHEN REQUEST FOR HEARING IS FILED AND THE ISSUE IS DISABILITY

Print, type or write clearly and answer all questions to the best of your ability. Complete answers will aid in processing the claim. IF ADDITIONAL SPACE IS NEEDED, ATTACH A SEPARATE STATEMENT TO THIS FORM.

CLAIMANT'S NAME	SOCIAL SECURITY NUMBER
WAGE EARNER (LEAVE BLANK IF NAME IS THE SAME AS THE CLAIMANT'S)	SOCIAL SECURITY NUMBER

PRIVACY ACT AND PAPERWORK ACT NOTICE: The Social Security Act (sections 205(a), 702, 1631(e)(1)(A) and (B), and 1869(b)(1) and (c), as appropriate authorizes the collection of information on this form. We will use the information on your recent activities, condition, medical treatment, and medications to help us decide if we need to obtain more information. You do not have to give it, but if you do not you may not receive benefits under the Social Security Act. We may give out the information on this form without your written consent if we need to get more information to decide if you are eligible for benefits or if a Federal law requires us to do so. Specifically, we may provide information to another Federal, State, or local government agency which is deciding your eligibility for a government benefit or program; to the President or a Congressman inquiring on your behalf; to an independent party who needs statistical information for a research paper or audit report on a Social Security program; or to the Department of Justice to represent the Federal Government in a court suit related to a program administered by the Social Security Administration.

We may also use the information you give us when we match records by computer. Matching programs compare our records with those of other Federal, State, or local government agencies. Many agencies may use matching programs to find or prove that a person qualifies for benefits paid by the Federal government. The law allows us to do this even if you do not agree to it.

These and other reasons why information about you may be used or given out are explained in the Federal Register. If you want to learn more about this, contact any Social Security Office.

TIME IT TAKES TO COMPLETE THIS FORM: We estimate that it will take you about 15 minutes to complete this form. This includes the time it will take to read the instructions, gather the necessary facts and fill out the form. If you have comments or suggestions on how long it takes to complete this form or on any other aspect of this form, write to the Social Security Administration. ATTN: Reports Clearance Officer, 1-A-21 Operations Bldg., Baltimore, MD 21235, and to the Office of Management and Budget, Paperwork Reduction Project (0960-0316), Washington, D.C. 20503. Do not send completed forms or information concerning your claim to these offices.

1. Have you worked since _____, the date your request for reconsideration was filed? (If yes, describe the nature and extent of work.) ☐ Yes ☐ No

2. Has there been any change in your condition since the above date? (If yes, describe the change.) ☐ Yes ☐ No

3. Have your daily activities and/or social functioning changed since the above date? (If yes, describe the changes.) ☐ Yes ☐ No

4. Have you been treated or examined by a doctor (other than as a patient in a hospital) since the above date? (If yes, complete the following.) ☐ Yes ☐ No

NAME AND ADDRESS OF DOCTOR(S)	DATE OF EXAM	MEDICAL PROBLEM

FORM **HA-4486** (9/90) (OVER)

Administrative Law Judge Appeal

5. Have you been a patient in a hospital since the above date? (If yes, complete the following.)		☐ Yes ☐ No
NAME AND ADDRESS OF HOSPITAL(S)	DATE OF HOSPITALIZATION	MEDICAL PROBLEM

6. Have you received medical or vocational services from a community agency since the above date? →	☐ Yes ☐ No

7. Are you now taking any prescription drugs or medications? (If yes, list them below.) →		☐ Yes ☐ No
NAME OF MEDICATION(S)	DOSAGE BEING TAKEN	NAME OF PHYSICIAN(S)

8. Are you now taking any nonprescription drugs or medications? (If yes, list them below.)	☐ Yes ☐ No
NAME OF MEDICATION(S)	DOSAGE BEING TAKEN

Knowing that anyone making a false statement or representation of a material fact for use in determining a right to payment under the Social Security Act commits a crime punishable under Federal Law, I certify that the above statements are true.

SIGNATURE OF CLAIMANT OR PERSON FILING ON THE CLAIMANT'S BEHALF	DATE SIGNED
SIGN HERE ▶	

Form HA-4486 (9/90)   *U.S. Government Printing Office: 1991 — 281-908/40066

EXHIBIT N

Authorization for Source to Release Information to the Social Security Administration (SSA)

RESIDENTS OF CALIFORNIA

I further authorize, by my signature below, a private photocopy company as approved by the Social Security Administration or the State Agency, to photocopy all medical records needed as evidence in determining my eligibility for SSA and/or SSI benefits. I also understand that I have a right to receive a copy of this authorization upon request. Copy requested and received.

☐ Yes ☐ No

TO BE COMPLETED BY SSA

NUMBER HOLDER

SOCIAL SECURITY NUMBER

EMPLOYEE/CLAIMANT/BENEFICIARY *(If other than Number Holder)*

AUTHORIZATION FOR SOURCE TO RELEASE INFORMATION TO THE SOCIAL SECURITY ADMINISTRATION (SSA)

INFORMATION ABOUT SOURCE — PLEASE PRINT, TYPE, OR WRITE CLEARLY

NAME AND ADDRESS OF SOURCE *(Include Zip Code)*	RELATIONSHIP TO CLAIMANT/BENEFICIARY

INFORMATION ABOUT CLAIMANT/BENEFICIARY — PLEASE PRINT, TYPE, OR WRITE CLEARLY

NAME AND ADDRESS *(If known)* AT TIME CLAIMANT/BENEFICIARY HAD CONTACT WITH SOURCE *(Include Zip Code)*	DATE OF BIRTH	CLAIMANT/BENEFICIARY I.D. NUMBER *(If known and different than SSN) (Clinic/Patient No.)*

APPROXIMATE DATES OF CLAIMANT/BENEFICIARY CONTACT WITH SOURCE *(e.g., dates of hospital admission, treatment, discharge, etc.)*

TO BE COMPLETED BY CLAIMANT/BENEFICIARY OR PERSON AUTHORIZED TO ACT IN HIS/HER BEHALF

GENERAL AND SPECIAL AUTHORIZATION TO RELEASE MEDICAL AND OTHER INFORMATION IN ACCORDANCE WITH THE PROVISIONS OF THE SOCIAL SECURITY ACT; THE PUBLIC HEALTH SERVICE ACT, SECTIONS 523 AND 527; AND TITLE 38 U.S.C. VETERANS BENEFITS, SECTION 4132.

I hereby authorize the above-named source to release or disclose to the Social Security Administration or State agency the following information for the period(s) identified above:

1) All medical records or other information regarding my treatment, hospitalization, and/or outpatient care for my impairment(s), including psychological or psychiatric impairment(s), drug abuse, alcoholism, sickle cell anemia, acquired immunodeficiency syndrome (AIDS), or tests for or infection with human immunodeficiency virus (HIV);

2) Information about how my impairment(s) affects my ability to complete tasks and activities of daily living;

3) Information about how my impairment(s) affected my ability to work.

I understand that this authorization, except for action already taken, may be voided by me at anytime. If I do not void this authorization, it will automatically end when a final decision is made on my claim. If I am already receiving benefits, the authorization will end when a final decision is made as to whether I can continue to receive benefits.

READ IMPORTANT INFORMATION ON REVERSE BEFORE SIGNING FORM BELOW.

SIGNATURE OF CLAIMANT/BENEFICIARY OR PERSON AUTHORIZED TO ACT IN HIS/HER BEHALF	RELATIONSHIP TO CLAIMANT/BENEFICIARY *(If other than self)*	DATE

STREET ADDRESS	TELEPHONE NUMBER *(Area Code)*

CITY	STATE	ZIP CODE

The signature and address of a person who either knows the person signing this form or is satisfifed as to that person's identity is requested below. This is not required by the Social Security Administration, but without it the source may not honor this authorization.

SIGNATURE OF WITNESS	STREET ADDRESS

CITY	STATE	ZIP CODE

Form SSA-827-OP1 (7-92) Use Prior Editions **(OVER)**

EXHIBIT O
Waiver of Right to Oral Hearing

I have been advised that I have the right to have an oral hearing and that this oral hearing will provide me with an opportunity to present witnesses and to explain in detail to the administrative law judge, who will make the decision in my case, the reasons why my case should be allowed. I understand that this opportunity to be seen and heard could be effective in explaining the facts in my case. (It could be especially useful in disability cases, since the administrative law judge would have an opportunity to hear an explanation as to how my impairments prevent me from working and restrict my activities.)[1]

I have been given an explanation of my right to representation, including representation at a hearing by an attorney or other person of my choice.

Although the above has been explained to me, I prefer to have my case decided on the evidence of record, plus any evidence which I may submit or which may be obtained by the social security office or the hearing office. I do not wish an oral hearing for the following reasons:

_____
_____
_____
_____
_____
_____
_____
_____
_____
_____
_____
_____
_____
_____
_____

I have been advised that, if I change my mind, I can request an oral hearing prior to mailing of the decision in my case. In this event I can make the request with the social security office or with the hearing office.

_____ _____
SIGNATURE OF CLAIMANT   DATE

[1] Note to social security office personnel: Where the issue to be decided is other than disability, the material in parentheses need not be discussed with the claimant.

Form HA-4608 (9-79) (Destroy Old Stock)

EXHIBIT P

Appointment of Representative

**DEPARTMENT OF
HEALTH AND HUMAN SERVICES
SOCIAL SECURITY ADMINISTRATION**

NAME (Claimant) (Print or Type)	SOCIAL SECURITY NUMBER
WAGE EARNER (if different)	SOCIAL SECURITY NUMBER

Section I APPOINTMENT OF REPRESENTATIVE

I appoint this individual _____
(Name and Address)

to act as my representative in connection with my claim or asserted right under:

☐ Title II (RSDI)   ☐ Title XVI (SSI)   ☐ Title IV FMSHA (Black Lung)   ☐ Title XVIII (Medicare Coverage)

I authorize this individual to make or give any request or notice; to present or elicit evidence; to obtain information; and to receive any notice in connection with my pending claim or asserted right wholly in my stead.

SIGNATURE (Claimant)	ADDRESS
TELEPHONE NUMBER	DATE
(Area Code)	

Section II ACCEPTANCE OF APPOINTMENT

I, _____ , hereby accept the above appointment. I certify that I have not been suspended or prohibited from practice before the Social Security Administration; that I am not, as a current or former officer or employee of the United States, disqualified from acting as the claimant's representative; and that I will not charge or receive any fee for the representation unless it has been authorized in accordance with the laws and regulations referred to on the reverse side hereof. In the event that I decide not to charge or collect a fee for the representation, I will notify the Social Security Administration. (Completion of Section III satisfies this requirement.)

I am a / an _____
(Attorney, union representative, relative, law student, etc.)

SIGNATURE (Representative)	ADDRESS
TELEPHONE NUMBER	DATE
(Area code)	

Section III (Optional) WAIVER OF FEE

I waive my right to charge and collect a fee under Section 206 of the Social Security Act, and I release my client (the claimant) from any obligations, contractual or otherwise, which may be owed to me for services I have performed in connection with my client's claim or asserted right.

SIGNATURE (Representative)	DATE

WAIVER OF DIRECT PAYMENT

I ONLY waive my right to direct certification of a fee from the withheld past-due benefits of my client (the claimant). I do NOT, however, waive my right to petition for and be authorized to charge and collect a fee directly from my client.

SIGNATURE (Representative)	DATE

Form SSA-1696-U4 (3-88)   *(See Important Information on Reverse)*   **FILE COPY**
Destroy prior editions

Bibliography

Office of the Federal Register, National Archives and Records Administration. *Code of Federal Regulations (CFR),* Book 20, Parts 404.101 to 404.2127, Parts 416.101 to 416.2227. Office of the Federal Register, April 1, 1995.

U.S. Department of Health and Human Services. *Social Security Handbook 1993 (CFR),* 11th ed. U.S. Department of Health and Human Services, Social Security Administration (SSA) Publication No. 65-008, August 1993. *(Available at Federal Depository libraries.)*

U.S. Department of Labor. *Dictionary of Occupational Titles,* 4th ed. 2 vols. U.S. Department of Labor, Employment and Training Administration, rev. 1991.

Index

Administrative Law Judge Appeal (ALJ), 3–4, 149–166
    application, 156
    Appointment of Representative form, 159, 166
    Authorization for Source to Release Information to the SSA form, 158, 164
    Claimant's Statement When Request for Hearing is Filed and the Issue is Disability form, 157–158, 162–163
    filing extention, 149
    financial problems, 155
    hearing, 151–155
    judge's decision, 159–160
    representation, 150–151
    Request for Hearing by Administrative Law Judge form, 157, 161
    SSA file, 153–154
    Waiver of Right to Oral Hearing form, 155, 158–159, 165
Adrenal Cortex Impairments, 32, 51
Adrenogenital Syndrome, 53
AIDS, 30
Alcoholism, 13, 82
ALJ (See "Administrative Law Judge Appeal")
Anemia, 28–29
Appeals
    ALJ, 3–4, 149–166
    reconsideration, 137–149
Applications
    ALJ, 156
    disability, 93–129 (See also "Disability Application")
Appointment of Representative Form (ALJ), 159, 166
Arthritis, 19–20, 41
Asthma, 44–45
Attorneys (See "Representation")

Authorization for Source to Release Information to the SSA Form
    ALJ, 158, 164
    reconsideration appeal, 141, 148

Blood Clotting Disorders, 29
Bowel Disease, Chronic Inflammatory, 47

Cancer, 38, 70–72
Case Reviews, 129
Cash Benefits, Special (SSI), 92
Cerebral Palsy, 34, 57
Checks (See "Payments")
Chest Pain Questionnaire (Disability Application), 101, 121–123
Children, Impairments, 39–72 (See also "Impairments")
Claimant's Statement When Request for Hearing is Filed and the Issue is Disability Form (ALJ), 157–158, 162–163
Coagulation Disorders, 29, 49
Colostomy, 25
Communication Impairments, 57
Concurrent Case, 2
Congenital Abnormalities, Catastrophic, 54–55
Consultative Exam Form (Disability Application), 95
Convulsive Disorders, 34–35
Cover Letters
    ALJ, 156
    disability application, 101, 102
    reconsideration appeal, 141–142
Criminal Convictions, 6
Cystic Fibrosis, 44

Daily Activities Questionnaire (Disability Application), 101, 124–127
DDS (See "Disability Determination Section")

Index

Deafness, 21
Deductions, Work Expense, 90–91
Denials, 3–4
Diabetes, 31, 32, 52
Disability Application
   Chest Pain Questionnaire, 101, 121–123
   claimant death, 8
   completing, 93–129
   Consultative Exam form, 95
   cover letter, 101, 102
   Daily Activities Questionnaire, 101,124–127
   Disability Appointment form, 95, 106
   Disability Report, 95–99, 108–113
   filing, 7
   form, 105
   Importance of Keeping a Medical Appointment form, 107
   Instruction Sheet, 94
   procedure, 3–4
   requirements, 7
   Seizure Questionnaire, 100, 120
   telephone interview, 102–104
   Vocational Report, 99–100, 114–119
Disability Appointment Form (Disability Application), 95, 106
Disability Determination Section (DDS), 3
Disability Determination, 5–6, 7–14
Disability Report (Disability Application), 95–99, 108–113
Diseases (See "Impairments")
Down's Syndrome, 54
Drug Addiction, SSI Eligibility, 82
Dysgammaglobulinemia/Hypogammaglobulinemia, 55

Earned Income, 85
Earnings Records, Correcting, 134–135
Emergency Advance Payments (SSI), 84–85
Eyes, Diseases/Injuries, 20

Filing Extensions
   ALJ, 149
   reconsideration appeal, 137–138
Financial Problems (ALJ), 155
Form 1099 (Social Security Benefit Statement), 132

Gastrointestinal Impairments, 47
Growth Impairments, 39–40

Hearing Impairments, 20, 43–44
Hearings (ALJ), 151–155
Heart Impairments, 23–24, 45–46

Hematologic Malignancies, 29
Hyperparathyroidism, 31, 51
Hypertensive Diseases, 23, 46
Hypogammaglobulinemia/Dysgammaglobulinemia, 55
Hypoparathyroidism/Pseudohypoparathyroidism, 31, 52

Iatrogenic Hypercorticoid State with Chronic Glucocorticoid Therapy, 52
Ileostomy, 25
Illnesses (See "Impairments")
Impairment–Related Work Expenses (IRWE), 91
Impairments, 15–38, 39–72
Income, SSI Eligibility, 85–86
Institutional Residents, SSI Eligibility, 80–81
Intestinal Impairments, 25
IRWE (See "Impairment-Related Work Expenses")

Kidney Disease, 27

Lawyers (See "Representation")
Letters, Cover
   ALJ, 156
   Disability Application, 101, 102
   reconsideration appeal, 141–142
Leukemia, 29, 50
Limbs, Upper and Lower, Fractures, 18
Liver Disease, 47
Low-Income Status, 134

Malnutrition, 25–26, 48
Medicaid/Medi-Cal, 81, 92, 132–134
Medical Evidence, 8–9
   alcoholism, 13
   medication, 12
   prescribed treatments, 12–13
   SSA medical appointments, 10–11
   symptoms, 11–12
Medical-Care Facility Residents, SSI Eligibility, 81
Medicare, 132
Mental Disorders, 35–38, 57–70
Motor Impairments, 55–57
Multiple Body Dysfunction, 54
Multiple Sclerosis, 34
Musculoskeletal Impairments, 17, 41
Myoclonic Seizures, 55

Nephritic Syndrome, 27
Neurohypophyseal Insufficiency, 31

Obesity, 32–33
Osteomyelitis, 42

PASS (See "Plans for Acheivng Self-Support")
Payee, Representative, 88–90
Payments, 84–86, 130–131
Penalties (SSI), 83
Personal Earnings and Benefit Estimate Statement, 135
Pituitary Dwarfism, 53
Plans for Acheiving Self-Support (PASS), 92
Presumptive Disability or Blindness (SSI), 83–84
Prison Convictions/Confinement, 6
Property (See "Resources")
Property Taxes, Assistance/Postponement Programs, 136
Pseudohypoparathyroidism/ Hypoparathyroidism, 31, 52
Pulmonary Impairments, 44

Reconsideration Appeal, 137–148
  Authorization for Source to Release Information to the SSA form, 141, 148
  cover letter, 141–142
  filing extension, 137–138
  Reconsideration Disability Report, 139–141, 144–147
  Request for Reconsideration form, 138–139, 143
Redetermination, SSI Eligibility, 82
Renal Impairments, 26–27, 48–49
Representation (ALJ), 150–151
Representative Payee, 88–90
Request for Hearing by Administrative Law Judge Form (ALJ), 157, 161
Request for Earnings and Benefit Estimate Statement (Form SSA-700 4SM), 135
Request for Reconsideration Form (Reconsideration appeal), 138–139, 143
Residual Functional Capacity (RFC), 6–7
Resources, SSI Eligibility, 86–88
Respiratory System Impairments, 22–23
Retirement Plans, Vested Right, 134
Reviews, Case, 129
RFC (See "Residual Functional Capacity")

Seizure Questionnaire (Disability Application), 100, 120
Seizures, 34, 55
SGA (See "Substantial Gainful Activity")
Sickle Cell Disease, 28–29, 49
Skin Disorders, 30

Social Security Benefit Statement (Form 1099), 132
Social Security Disability Insurance (SSDI), 1–2
Spine, disorders of, 17–18, 41–42
SSA file (ALJ), 153–154
SSDI (See "Social Security Disability Insurance")
SSI (See "Supplemental Security Income Program")
State disability benefits, 4
Status change reports (SSI), 83
Substantial gainful activity (SGA), 5–6
Supplemental Security Income Program (SSI), 1–2, 79–92
  cash benefits, special, 92
  eligibility, 79–81
  emergency advance payments, 84–85
  income, 85–86
  penalties, 83
  presumptive disability/blindness, 83–84
  redetermination, 82
  representative payee, 88–90
  required information, 83
  resources, 86–88
  work incentive programs, 90–92

Taxes, Property, Assistance/Postponement Programs, 136
Telephone Interview (Disability Application), 102–104
Thyroid Disorder, 31
Title II Program (See "Supplemental Security Disability Insurance")
Title XVI Program (See "Supplemental Security Income")

Ulcers, 25
Unearned Income, 86

Vertigo, 21
Vestibular Disorder, 21–22
Visual Impairments, 42–43
Vocational Rehabilitation Services
  extended benefits, 91
  SSI eligibility, 81–82
Vocational Report (Disability Application), 99–100, 114–119

Waiver of Right to Oral Hearing form (ALJ), 155, 158–159, 165
Work, 73–78, 90–92
Worker's Compensation Benefits, 4